NEXT TIME AROUND

NEXT TIME AROUND

Some Things Pleasantly Remembered

BY JOHN GOULD

Illustrations by Consuelo Eames Hanks

W · W · NORTON & COMPANY
NEW YORK   LONDON

Copyright © 1983 by John Gould
All rights reserved.
Published simultaneously in Canada by
George J. McLeod Limited, Toronto.
Printed in the United States of America.

The text of this book is composed in Palatino,
with display type set in Palatino.
Composition and manufacturing by
The Maple-Vail Book Manufacturing Group.
Book design by Holly McNeely.

First Edition

Library of Congress Cataloging in Publication Data
Gould, John, 1908–
Next time around.
1. Gould, John, 1908— Autobiography.   2. Authors,
American—20th century—Autobiography.   3. Maine—Social
life and customs.   I. Title.
PS3513.O852Z473   1983   818'.5209 [B]   83-4092

ISBN 0-393-01777-X

W. W. Norton & Company, Inc.
500 Fifth Avenue, New York, N.Y. 10110

W. W. Norton & Company Ltd.
37 Great Russell Street, London WC1B 3NU

1 2 3 4 5 6 7 8 9 0

FOR WILLIAM DORNBUSCH

Who is the grandfather
of my two grandsons

The next thing most like living one's life over again seems to be a recollection of that life, and to make that recollection as durable as possible by putting it down in writing.

—Benjamin Franklin

Which sounds to me
Like déjà vu.
(Signed) Peter Partout
(Friend of the family)

Peppermint Corner, Maine

NEXT TIME AROUND

ONE

Stanley Simmons is a Maine lobsterman, and reasonably typical. He fishes down Muscongus Bay out of Friendship harbor, as do some three hundred other Friendshippers, and while he wouldn't take up any other trade, profession, and labor if you clapped a pistol to his head, he down-speaks lobstering as a matter of tradition. Nothing ever goes right for the lobster catcher—he'll tell you. It's a hard life. I can't remember a lobsterman who seemed unhappy, or looked unprosperous, but all of them protest the weather, the expenses, the scarcity of "counters" (legal keepers), the evil buyers and wholesalers, the summer mahogany (yachters), and the seasonal resident. Stanley, dry smoking a lightly corned cigar, will express the constant negative opinion with as eloquent a "Daow!" as you'll hear from Pull-and-be-damned Point to the Passamaquoddy, but on every topic except lobstering his remarks are rational, pleasant, witty, and always worth hearing. His ready answer to the trick, or unexpected, question endeared him to me in the early days of our friendship, and I used to try him out. He's never failed me yet.

There was a brilliant July day with maybe fifty or seventy-five tourists (we call 'em "summer complaints") standing on the buyer's wharf, looking down on the float where the fishermen were weighing in the day's haul. These fishermen had been out since daybreak, and tied up at the float one by one just long enough to sell their catch, take on bait and fuel for tomorrow, and fold their payments into their hip pockets. This procession makes a dandy show for the summer people, but none of the lobstermen thus performing ever shows that he is aware of an audience. I chanced along just as Stanley tied up and began passing over his catch; one in each hand, two at a time, he picked them from his tanks and laid them in the buyer's crates. Stan had done well that morning. It took a little time. He paused as one crate went to the platform scales and before he began to fill another. Fifteen feet down, on a low tide, Stan may or may not have known that the wharf was loaded with people admiring this scene. Almost everybody was clicking a camera.

"Stan!" I yelled, and Stan didn't know who yelled or what was coming.

He looked up, long-billed swordfish cap and his dry cigar, and he didn't single me out in the crowd. "Eyah?" he said. He still didn't know who had called to him.

"You want to preach for me again this Sunday?"

Not the slightest pause. Didn't faze him, as we say. "That's up to Vassalborough?"

"Eyah," I said.

"O.K.," said Stan, and he turned back to handling his lobsters, and the crowd on the wharf was utterly silent.

We wondered if any of the summer complaints went up to Vassalborough that Sunday to hunt up any church services. The tilt did give some of us an esoteric outcome—there is a small tendency in Friendship to keep the whimsey alive. Now and then somebody will ask Stan if he took up a good collection last Sunday, and he always has an answer to that, too.

I mention Stan now because of something he said one other day. Things really hadn't been all that lucky. A storm had made a mess down the bay and a good many traps had been lost. The wind kept up, so the men couldn't go to see about the damage and their losses. The price had, of course, gone up because of short supply, and there was no way to take advantage of this. Stan was headed to put his boat on her mooring, calling it quits for another lackluster day, and he chugged slowly by as I stood on the pier. "Next time around," he shouted, "I'm going to do something else!"

Maybe.

I went to my bookshelf afterwards and took down Nathaniel Hawthorne, to look again at his tale "Dr. Heidegger's Experiment." Here, Dr. Heidegger plies four old folks with the elixir of the Fountain of Youth and watches them become young again. I hadn't looked at Hawthorne for some time, and was much taken with his choral remarks. For instance:

"Give us more of this wondrous water!" cried they, eagerly. "We are younger,—but we are still too old! Quick— give us more!"

You don't hear four people all talking together that way too often. The story shows that when given a chance to live a life again folks won't be much different. These four, rejuvenated, start repeating themselves, and probably if Stanley Simmons were to have a second time around, he would be the same Stanley Simmons, lobster catcher. True, with his ready tongue he might make a passable preacher, at least on the Vassalborough level, but when we ask him about the Sunday collections some of his answers indicate that he is not basically ready for the pulpit.

Meantime, what is wrong with doing some things again? On another time around, I would like to have a second crack at a number of good memories.

TWO

Food, I was told long ago, is a foolproof topic. Everybody eats. Some people do not play golf; some do not angle; some do not attend church; some never marry; some won't smoke and roister. But hunger creeps up on us all, and an essay about something to eat is a winner. With a difference—many editors, publishers, and writers abuse this truth. It is not enough to turn loose a woman who has a dossier of seasonal recipes and call the result a food page. Household pages tend to be dull; good food should be attended by good writing. Much of our culinary literature attracts no more attention than do nuts and bolts and how-to stories about a leaky faucet. One of the most prolonged spates of letters-to-the-editor in the history of American journalism had to do with red flannel hash. For over a month the mail came by bags and bags. This was prompted by a jaunty but not weighty item on the subject, and the editors were dismayed—their hefty opinions about the United Nations and Human Rights ought, don't you think, to be much more important than a hash made of corned beef and beets? But it is not so, and if you'll let me have the mince pies and shore-boiled lobsters, I care not who makes the nation's songs.

I have dined well. My mother and my wife's mother served cookstove apprenticeships in the down-east Maritimes, where basic meat and potatoes are cunningly fabricated into plain food that causes the children to believe they grew up as millionaires. In her turn, my wife has given me no cause to complain. I have been to foreign places and have frequented fine restaurants. And my remarks about baked beans, apple pies, and suchlike sundries are in numerous anthologies. If, on a second time around, I might repeat my favorite, I would ask for a certain breakfast we had soon after we were married, before our house was built, when we were living stoically in our log cabin.

We slept up in a loft there, gained by a ladder, which was the way in pioneer times. The two double beds were right under the roof, and in winter this was fine. Heat rises, and as our cabin cooled down and the fire in the heater went to embers, it stayed comfortable aloft. On real cold nights I'd limber down the ladder a couple of times and restoke, but if the weather softened we were good until daybreak. We had, the evening before this memorable breakfast, taken our supper, stoked the stove, extinguished the cat, and climbed up to our rest. As I assisted the cat in his departure, I noticed that the stars were crystal bright in the chill Maine sky, and that Lisbon Ridge continued to survey the eastern valley in its customary agreeable manner. I could see the lights of the village, and just before I closed the door I heard a freight train on the main line blow for the Fisher Road crossing. It wasn't every night we could hear the whistle at that distance; only when the air was still and cold. As I did every night, I shut the door and smiled at the absurdity of the bolt. There was the bolt, mounted on the door when the cabin was built, and it had never been shot. When we went away, we would lock the door from outside with a padlock, but we had never fastened it from the inside. Down in the city my wife's parents never went to bed without locking both the front and the back doors, checking the bar on the cellarway and the fastenings on the windows, so we had a routine we went through. Every night after the cat was gone, she'd ask, "Are you sure you locked up?"

"Yes," I would answer. "All secure!" And there was the bolt unbolted, and anybody, friend or foe, might have come in. But on the farm there are no foes. Thus it was.

Owen Gilman was a college classmate, and as two G's we sat in adjacent chairs in a number of Latin classes. College associations don't usually last, but Owen and I have remained close these fifty years. Sometimes the Gilmans came to see us, and again we would visit them at the cottage on Clearwater Pond— in the town of Industry, not far above Farmington. Clearwater, as a name, was the nicety introduced by the seasonal colony. Quite a few places in Maine experienced similar improvements. Dry Pond, after city folks put up their summer places, became Crystal Lake. Hardscrabble Road is now Dennison Avenue. Things like that. Skunk's Misery is Birchvista. And Clearwater

Pond used to be Bull Horse Pond. The Gilmans, being people, refused to recognize "Clearwater," and continued to say "Bull Horse." This is important, since the chemical laboratory they operated in a corner of their woodshed produced, to the exclusion of all else, a refreshing beverage always spoken of as Bull Horse Pond Dew. Like wines and cheeses of note, Bull Horse Pond Dew could not be compounded anywhere else, and for quality, flavor, and popularity its like has not been produced. I should add, I suppose, that in its first days Bull Horse Pond Dew was illegal.

In our holidays with the Gilmans we came to know a number of Farmington people, among them the Titcombs. Clarence and Esther Titcomb operated a dairy farm on Titcomb Hill, with delivery routes around Franklin County. They also had a considerable maple syrup operation. They, the Gilmans, and we were congenial, and the six of us shared many good things, among them the time we coasted off Titcomb Hill on a bobsled in the moonlight and came within an ace of killing everybody in Farmington.

Soon after that, Owen became manager of the Farmington Farmers' Union. Here and there a farmers' union hangs on, but mostly they are part of history. On the co-op idea, they served farming communities and in their time served well. So Owen and Clarence got together on the matter of supplying feed for the Titcomb cattle. Clarence bought a lot of feed, and Owen thought he could get him a better price. In pursuit of this, they came down to Portland in Clarence's pickup truck to consult wholesalers and brokers. Inasmuch as neither had ever, in the wildest flight of possibility, thought one bit about embracing "Clearwater," the efficacy they brought to sustain them on this journey was Bull Horse Pond you-know-what. I'm sure Owen will not chide me for revealing this, and Clarence can't—he died a few years later in a tragic hunting accident. Woodswise to the hilt, he nevertheless pulled his deer rifle through a fence. But to resume . . .

They had consulted the wholesalers and brokers, who unanimously agreed that Bull Horse Pond Dew is remarkable, and that Clarence was paying too much for his feed. Just before time for the stores to close, Clarence and Owen went into Shaw's Market to stock up with groceries and provisions that would not be found in the stores at Farmington. Among these were thirty pounds of lamb chops, which Clarence meant to hold in his dairy cold box until occasion arose. The two then started their long trip home, and for my part I was not expecting them to detour in my vicinity.

We had supper, I put out the cat, and my wife asked, "Are you sure you locked up?" Up the ladder, we were soon in repose, something easy to gain with country air and clean living.

I was never able to bring Clarence and Owen to account for the several hours between their acquiring the lamb chops and their arrival at our cabin. Owen thought they came by way of South Paris, but Clarence distinctly remembered Harpswell. Their pickup bounded into our bucolic dooryard like a flatcar of pig iron being humped in the Richmond marshaling yards, and this success was celebrated by a thirteen-minute toot on the horn.

"What's THAT?" said my wife.

"What's what?" I answered. I squirted my flashlight from the loft towards the door, spotlighting the two gentlemen as they came in—Owen with a basket of large green bottles and Clarence with a box containing thirty pounds of lamb chops.

We were glad to see them and arose to the occasion. Dorothy wrapped up in her peignoir before advancing to buss our welcome and willing guests, but I made full preparations and dressed all the way. Owen began laying a fire in the cookstove, and Clarence opened the cupboard and started to set the table.

The steeple clock on our fireplace mantel said 2:45, and that was A.M.

Dorothy said, "Potatoes, apples, strawberries."

Good stories need narrative speed, and you will see that much has happened since the toot in the dooryard. If this occasion might be repeated on another time around, it should have the same pace; when Dorothy said, "Potatoes, apples, strawber-

ries," I had already opened the trap door to our vegetable cellar. I put some Green Mountains in a pail, filled it with Northern Spies, and picked two quart jars of preserved wild strawberries off a shelf. We didn't have a freezer until some years later.

Many hands make light work. Dorothy started the yeast rolls, and Owen peeled potatoes. I got the apples ready for a pie, and then sliced the potatoes for French fries. Clarence boned the lamb chops until he had a cookie sheet of them, and he wrapped each with bacon and thrust home a toothpick. A baker sheet of lamb chops hunter-style is a brave sight, and we admired it in reverence. The range had not yet brought the oven up to hot, so we permitted Owen to tell us again about the secret of Bull Horse Pond Dew and how it needs to be set in the dark of the moon.

Dorothy now had the two apple pies under construction, and the French-fry pot was beginning to smoke on the top of the stove. Clarence delivered an oration in which he said that hunter-style lamb chops also have a secret, and now the oven was ready. Dear Friends—I have watched Julia Child prepare endive and make drop cookies with peanut butter and chocolate chips. I'm talking about *food.* The orient sun was about to look over the rim of the Bowdoin Ridge and peek in at our cabin window when we took our places for breakfast. We had green peas, but they were from a can and had been brought to titillation by a cut of salt pork. We had the French fries, and we had the half acre of hunter-style lamb chops. We had yeast rolls. We had strawberry shortcake with the alternative of apple pie, or both. We had a pot of lumber-camp tea for all present who didn't care for Bull Horse Pond Dew. We had cultural conversations and philosophical deliberations. None of this has ever been on television or in a household section. The reluctant dawn of a Maine winter was now full upon us, and we diligently plied our silverware in the rosy glow of a glad new day in a happy world.

"I do hate to bring these devotions to an early halt," said Clarence, "but I'm due on Titcomb Hill to start the milking."

"Don't bother with the dishes," said Dorothy. "I've got all day."

In programming a second time around: We would still not use all the lamb chops, just the same glorious baker sheet of them, and Clarence would take the rest home. But we would finish the shortcake and the two pies.

THREE

G us Garcelon, the tooth carpenter, and I always tried to get away for a couple of days every fall, and some years we'd get our deer and some years we wouldn't see anything. It was extra fun to go into the woods with Gus because he was a gun buff, a real big shot in the National Rifle Association, and he could take a medal at any national shoot-out. And, which I've noticed is not usual with many of that sort, he was woodswise and a successful hunter. One year we started out on opening day—the day the law "goes off"—and we were heading for the Scott Brook lumber camp, where Del Bates, the clerk, was keeping a choppers' camp warm for us. This took us past the home of another good friend, old Flats Jackson. We wanted to be at Scott Brook by noon, so it was going on breakfast time when we got to the house of Flats. It would be a natural surmise that at breakfast time on opening day Flats would already have tagged a deer for himself, his wife Giselle, his son Bennie, Bennie's wife Bonnie, and one to grow on. Flats is the best woodsman I know, and has been known to open a season early.

We pulled into the dooryard to make a passing call, went in the back door, and found Beautiful Giselle frying liver and bacon. Flats was sitting a-wait at the kitchen table with a bottle of beer. It was 7:45 A.M. We made our greetings, and while Flats poured some beers Giselle sliced more liver and put a pan of biscuits in the oven. "Did you get your deer yet?" is the way we begin Maine conversations at that season, so I said, "Did you get your deer yet?" The liver that Giselle was slicing seemed to me to be a crystal-clear answer to my question.

Giselle now burst into uncontrolled hysterics and leaned against the wall until the spasm passed. "Did he *ever* get his deer!" she choked, and kept on laughing.

Flats just said "Eyah," and drew at his beer. Then he seemed to decide that he might just as well explain things, and he tilted back in his chair, linked his fingers behind his head, and spoke pretty much as follows: "Gizzie's jeezly brother from Uh-hi-uh come on two weeks ago and wanted a deer, so I took him over the mountain and set him on a stump and told him to keep his eyeballs on the downhill side but not to shoot at anything wearing a hat. He knows full as much about the woods as the Queen of England knows about poverty, and I sure wanted to know where he was if I was about to drive him a deer. So he promised to stay on the stump, and I circled down into Bugaboo Swamp and it wasn't too long before I jumped some game. He had my gun, and where I'd already got my deer, I didn't need a gun, and I didn't need to see the deer, either. So up over the hill goes what I supposed was a deer, a regular freight train in the puckerbrush, and headed right for that stump. I took my time starting up after, and all at once Gizzie's jeezly brother, name of Ned, opens up and he empties the magazine of my .30-30, and when the last cartridge quit, the ensuing silence was monumental."

Flats paused to permit general appreciation of his able rhetoric, unclasped his hands, drew again on his beer, and was about to resume his recitation when Giselle said "There! If you can eat more than that, let me know—I'll go start my housework." She hefted a platter of venison liver to the table, dumped out the biscuits, and poured camp coffee.

She went out of the kitchen, we fell to, and Flats continued: "It took me a few minutes to get out of the swamp, and I came up the rise to find Gizzie's jeezly brother right on that stump, obeying me to the hilt, and his eyes were glazed and dreamy and you could smell gunpowder as if the Battle of Bunker Hill was afoot. Take some more liver and hand me the plate. So— cuss't if he hadn't got himself seven deer. Two does, four bucks, and a spikehorn. Every one a clean shot. And there we were. He comes out of shock after a few minutes, and he goes over and puts his tag on the big buck—a real old rauncher—and that's the one he's going to take back to Uh-hi-uh. Beautiful rack; it must have gone about two hundred twelve and a half pounds dressed out. And now, you might say, there was I, forty miles from Halifax and a dead horse."

"And a dead horse?" said Gus. "What's a dead horse all about?"

Flats pours us more coffee and goes on: "Way of speaking. Fellow down in Nova Scotia was teaming a load of logs into Halifax when a snowstorm hit, and before too long the horses were bogged down in the snow up to their withers. Planning to encourage his team, this fellow brings a pole from a fence and belted one of the horses with it. Story goes the fellow said, 'I fetched him a humper with a longer and he fell kerjingling in the shafters, and there was I—forty miles from Halifax and a dead horse!' "

"And . . . ?" says Gus.

Flats meditated briefly, and then: "Sort of points up the folly of a rash plan. Here's this jeezly brother of Gizzie's about to head home all safe and secure, and there was I with a half a ton of meat that was as illegal as fornicating in church, and for once in my life I hadn't done anything wrong."

Gus said, "How did all this work out?"

"All right," said Flats. "He had to wait for the law to go off before he could move his buck, and he took off at daybreak this morning. Been cold weather, so we didn't lose any meat. I went into the Christmas tree business, is what I did. I'd go over on the mountain and cut a pickup load of Christmas trees, pile 'em on top of a deer, and come home. Got sixty dollars for the trees."

Flats pushed back his chair and stood up. "Come on," he said, "and see what I've got down sulla!" He opened the cellarway door and stood back so Gus and then I could pass in front of him. He fell on behind, all three of us going down at once.

Well, we found out what Flats had down cellar. Giselle, after she'd left us in the kitchen, had gathered up the week's wash and had gone down cellar to heave everything into the washing machine. She had dumped in the right amount of soap, turned on the power, and as the tub began to fill with water she lifted off her sweatshirt, stepped out of her jeans, and added these two basic garments to the laundry. She meant to turn around and take some clean clothes off a rack behind her, but she hadn't gone that far yet. There she was, as we came down, full naked, and looking into the washing machine as if it might be a TV set. Gus backed up, which caused me to back up, which caused Flats to back up, and this made something of a hooraw, with Flats on the kitchen floor and Gus and me on top of him. The commotion brought Giselle from her reverie and she came up to see what was going on, but not until she got into some clothes.

Then we went down and inspected the six deer. Flats was planning to skin them out and cut them up that day, so he excused himself and said he guessed he wouldn't go into Scott Brook with us. He said for us to convey his best to Del Bates.

I've included this in my list of things to do again on another time around.

FOUR

Once and only once in the first time around was I asked to perform as master of ceremonies for an annual meeting of the Androscoggin County Fish & Game Association. This was the largest sportsmen's organization in Maine. I lived in Androscoggin County but I was not a member. Amel Kizonak, who was a member, lived neighbor to me, and we had often been hunting and fishing companions. Amel had ambitions to become commissioner of inland fisheries and game for the State of Maine, and was using this association as a step of the ladder up. He got himself elected president of the Androscoggin County Fish & Game Association, and the big membership was a substantial boost to Amel's chances. He accordingly planned a bigger and better annual meeting with ladies' night and asked me to come and conduct the festivities. For Amel, yes.

Mostly from the Lewiston-Auburn area, the membership came to several hundred people, and with the women we filled the armory. The supper was the usual baked beans with ham and hot biscuits, choice of pies, and coffee. The crusty veteran bean pots were set right on the tables, piping hot, so people went looking into the pots to decide where to sit—to each his own kind. Amel and his committee had sandbagged all the merchants and mills and had a heap of door prizes. Everybody put his ticket in a box, and we had the current Miss Maine to reach in and pull out winners. Amel also had a good list of people who would say a few words. I called on a clergyman to offer a blessing, and supper began. Every few minutes we'd draw a winner and award a door prize, and after the food was gone I'd introduce somebody between each drawing.

Now, since Amel had his sights on the commissionership, it was a bit sticky as concerned the incumbent. The commissioner of inland fisheries and game had indeed been invited to attend, but he was not about to lend his dignity to anything that would make Amel look good, and Amel had not expected him to come. That particular commissioner was not much given to making appearances anyway. Sportsmen complained that he was hard to see, and didn't even come to the hearings he called. This complaining was good for Amel. However, the annual meeting of the Androscoggin County Fish & Game Association was something the commissioner of inland fisheries and game could not judiciously ignore. Under the circumstances, he sent his deputy commissioner to represent him.

This was a mistake. The deputy was a stuffed shirt, completely in disrepute with every sportsman in Maine. And here he was at the head table—an insult, in the eyes of every member, to Amel, their fair-haired boy. And, being a jerk, he compounded his disadvantage. When he came in, he told me privately that his appearance was purely official, that he was representing the commissioner out of courtesy, and that considering everything, he did not care to be called on for remarks. "I'll just take a bow," he said.

What a thing! Here was a fun time, an eat-and-cheer evening, with a boat and motor coming up as the farewell door prize! It was not a time to take too much of anything seriously. Nobody expected the deputy commissioner to make extended and ponderous remarks. But he certainly should commend the association for a good turnout and a good supper, and assure the members the department was aware of their interests. Maybe he could tell a joke. But something, anyway. Nope. Just a bow. As the program went along I meditated on these things, and now it came time for me to introduce the deputy commissioner of the Department of Inland Fisheries and Game, who would ordinarily (I said) bring us greetings from the commissioner himself, who had found it impossible to be with us tonight. But (I said), the deputy had asked to be relieved of any remarks, and had expressed a wish merely to take a bow. The deputy looked up at me as if to commend me for obliging him, and also as if to assure me he was ready for his bow.

I'm going to tell you exactly what I said next.

I said, "However, if anybody from the State House thinks he can come down here and eat our Androscoggin County baked beans without rendering a report, he will find he's mistaken."

The place came down, so to speak. We made the drawing on the boat and motor, and the laughter kept on. Soon the deputy excused himself, and he was given a magnificent burst of applause as he walked out. Amel wasn't at all pleased with me, and didn't speak for months. I was never asked to appear again at the meetings of the Androscoggin County Fish & Game Association, but I'm told that the older members still chuckle in the memory of the time I did attend. Amel, by the way, never made it to the top. There may have been something in his politicking that hindered his appointment. Perhaps on another time around I would be more discreet and help his chances.

FIVE

M r. Sorensen was a Swede, which is merely to say that in
our down-Maine Yankee town he was an odd one. So
he was suspicious when my father approached him with a proposition. Mr. Sorensen had a wood lot up on the Woodchuck
Road, running to hard wood that was ready to cut. My father,
at the time, did not have a wood lot, so he suggested to Mr.
Sorensen that some chopping be done "on the halves." This is
a long-standing State-o'-Maine arrangement—one man cuts on
the other man's land, and cord for cord they divide the harvest.
Mr. Sorensen had never heard of this, so he shook his head and
said he would think it over. My father came home thinking this
reluctance amounted to a refusal.

The wood lot is on its own second time around. Coal and then
oil took over, and the woodshed that went with every home
served no purpose for many years. Now, wood is looking good
again and the old Maine custom of cutting on the halves is again
in good style. The wood-burning stove that my father wanted
to feed with Mr. Sorensen's wood was the "black mogul" of my
mother's kitchen in my boyhood.

About two weeks later Mr. Sorensen drove his stringy white
horse into our yard, carefully alighted from the rim-wracked
buggy, and came to the door. "Ay tank dat's goo-ood plan," he
told my father, and every Saturday that was decent that winter
my father and I walked to the Sorensen lot and chopped cordwood on the halves. We learned later that Mr. Sorensen had not
understood the expression, and had gone to our local lawyer to
ask about the validity of this strange Yankee bargain. The lawyer assured him it was an accepted Maine custom, and that with
my father it was "as good as wheat." It was equally good with
Mr. Sorensen. He would come now and then to get the wood
we had piled for him, and over and above the bargain he would

come with his white horse and haul ours. I'd come home from weekday school to find the pile in our yard extended, and by spring it was a substantial quantity.

Today, if I cut any wood, I do it with a chain saw and haul it with a tractor. Nobody is going to relive those Saturdays when Dad and I took a lunch and walked cross-lots to Mr. Sorensen's lot—about a mile. We each had an ax, but mine was still a boy's ax and I was still a boy. We had, also, an obsolete tool known as a one-man crosscut saw. The real crosscut saw had a handle on each end, and two men drew it back and forth. The steel was fairly limber. Made of stiffer steel, and therefor heavier, the one-man crosscut was by no means as efficient a tool, but a man working alone could get some wood out. Also, a handle could be fitted on the off end so the one-man could be used as a two-man. (I still have Dad's one-man saw hanging on my shop wall, but it hasn't been off the nail in fifty years.) I pulled on the off end, with Dad doing the real work, and he used to say that he didn't mind my riding back and forth, but he wished I wouldn't drag my feet. We went for maples, mostly, about ten inches DBH (that's diameter breast high), and after enough yanking on the saw we'd fell one, and limb it out with our axes. Then we'd make the log into four-foot cordwood and pile it in two piles. Piling brought the Saturday afternoon to an end, and the winter days were short. It would be dark when we came out of the wood lot and started for home, where the kitchen window would be alight and Mother would be making supper.

You can't go back and do it again. We had a potato basket— this is a basket made by the Micmac Indians for gathering potatoes in Aroostook County. Mother would lay our Saturday lunch into that. There was no plastic and cellophane then, and we had to bring home the cloth napkins in which she wrapped the food. When we set forth, Dad and I would walk abreast, each with a hand to the basket, but he would carry it alone where we had to walk single-file. Our first duty after reaching the wood lot was to kindle a small fire, and we kept it going all morning so our lunch wouldn't freeze. After the first Saturday, we left our tools at the lot, hidden so rabbit hunters wouldn't find them, and we took them home only when they needed sharpening. One Saturday a new snow changed the appearance of things, and after we got a fire started we couldn't find our tools ourselves. We tromped around and hunted for an hour and there they were. After that we always broke a twig to mark the place. And after the snow built up, we had enough limbs on the ground so the rabbits really moved in. They'd eat the tips. I told Mother, back at the house, that we had a zillion bunnies. Dad cautioned me not to get overeager about estimating wildlife—people brag that they saw fifteen deer, whereas they saw one deer fifteen times. But it did seem to me we had a lot of rabbits—the big variable hares, the snowshoe rabbits. Dad let me take my .22, and I became a meat hunter. He allowed me two shots a Saturday and that's all. If I missed, too bad. If I got two rabbits, and I usually did, we'd dress them out and let them freeze, and we'd carry them home in the potato basket. Mother made excellent rabbit pies.

She also put up good choppers' dinners. We'd stir up the little fire and sit across from each other in its comfort. We had good days and we had snowstorms, but sometimes the wind made us quit early. Dad would boil a can of tea over the fire, and when it was ready we'd unwrap the basket goodies and have a feast. There was always an apple pie. And there was always Dad's philosophizin' and yarnin', and never a noonin' that wasn't worth having again.

Excellent as it always was, our sumptous banquet by the fire in the Sorensen wood lot was not the big meal of the day. When we dragged home, dog-tired, the empty basket swinging over an arm, we were hungry again. Stomp the snow off on the porch, sweep the boots with the broom, reach for the doorknob. Out would burst the pent-up delight of the day's effort in the kitchen. A mixture of new bread, apple pies, cakes, baking beans, and the steam from the brown bread. There would be cookies and doughnuts and gingerbreads, too, and my eyes have just clouded over at the thought. . . . .

Best route to supper is through a wood lot, my father said many times. He'd cross to the rocker by the stove and put a foot up on the hearth to begin taking off a boot. I did the same from a stool by the pantry door. Wash-up at the sink, side by side, man and boy, and Mother would have the cooking dishes pushed aside so our basins were ready. Then the roller towel—low down for me but higher up for Dad. "Ready?" Mother would ask.

Ready! "Please pass the beans," Dad would say, and he wasn't even at the table yet.

SIX

When our children came to that special time in high school when they went on their "class ride," the Mothers' Club raised the money and they took the tour-guided bus to Washington, D.C. They met our senators, saw the monuments, took a quick pass through the Smithsonian, and paused in New York on the way home. This, to me, is a newer kind of class ride, and I made no effort at the time to tell my youngsters how Peggy Day fell in the brook.

There was no Mothers' Club needed in the early years of my new century, because financing the trip came to just fifty cents. Not apiece, but for the couple. Having found his fifty cents, a boy could safely invite a girl to be his partner, and she was expected to bring the lunch. The fifty cents, in my town, went to Edgar Conant, who provided hayracks, horses, and drivers. That was it. It took three hayracks to accommodate our whole school, including the chaperons. The particular ride I speak of, involving Peggy, went six miles out to Quaker Meeting House, by way of Ward Town, where we had our picnic in the moonlight, around a bonfire, and then returned to town soon after midnight by the back road and Beech Hill. Ethelyn Davis had brought my lunch, and Peggy had brought one for Eddie Skillin, and we four were in the forward hayrack, which was being driven by Milt Dill and had as chaperon Margaret Ashworth, our English teacher.

Miss Ashworth was not up on the seat with Milt, where chaperons usually performed, and for good reason. As the October evening of the full moon was sharp, Milt had broken out his teamster's buffalo coat—a furry and redolent relic of many years around the Conant stables, assurance enough that Milt would ride alone. So with Miss Ashworth truly in our midst, we snuggled under blankets in the loose hay, and singing, off we went.

34

Sometimes a ride would be on snow and runners, but this one was on wheels. Tailgating, the three racks passed from the last streetlight of the village into the darkness beyond, and the words we sang ran:

Ready all to shout the call for F. H. S.,
Loud and high ring out the cry for F. H. S.,
Clear the way, prepare the fray for F.— H.— S.—
We are marching on to
VICT-TOR-REEEEEE!

Thus we came to approach Quaker Meeting House, where an advance committee would have a fire kindled. Now, a glad and wandering couple from one of the other racks climbed over our rail and tumbled amongst us. It was all right to visit back and forth, so Peggy Day and Eddie Skillin took a mind to leave us and go see what went on elsewhere. Over the side they went, Eddie first, and with a whoop he dropped to the side of the dirt roadway below. With another whoop, Peggy let go and meant to join him. But in that small time between the two departures, Miltie's horses had plodded ahead onto a bridge, and Peggy went down about fifteen feet into Farwell's brook. There was a crimson squeal the full distance, then a magnificent splash, and silence. Miltie said "Whoa," and then added, "Don't nob'dy get off the side. Get off on back. We're on a bridge!"

"Get off the back end!" added Miss Ashworth.

Peggy was unhurt in every particular except her dignity. She was chilled, and Miss Ashworth told her to run for the bonfire, which wasn't too far up the road. With a girl on each arm, Peggy struck out in the night, and when the rest of us came along with the hayracks, there was Peggy, stripped, agleam in the glow of the bonfire, her cast-off garments beginning to steam as the girls held them on sticks toward the blaze. Miss Ashworth was fairly swift, but it does take a little time to dismount a schoolmarm from a hayrack, and by the time she got a blanket wrapped around Peggy . . . Then all the girls crowded in to form a pali-

35

sade, and we boys were on our own. Lunch was delayed until Peggy's clothes were dry. So was our arrival back in town, and it was graying in the east when we came to the first streetlight.

As I say—I didn't try to tell my own children what a class ride should really be all about. I contributed some cash, and let 'em go on the bus to Washington, where they saw many wonderful sights.

SEVEN

I ntroducing somebody "from away" to the playful esoterics of
the State o' Maine makes a pleasant moment and should
happen more often. I'd like to rerun the time Colonel John Lee
passed the chain at Daaquam, on the International Paper Company private logging road to Clayton Lake. Colonel Lee is a fine
man, full worthy of the honor played upon him, and he stayed
mad only an hour or so. I was never told how Mr. Lee obtained
his rank, and it may have been for valor under fire. At first I
took him for one of those Kentucky colonels, and I showed him
my commission as an admiral in the Great Navy of the State of
Nebraska. I keep the card in my wallet for deflationary purposes
and it comes in handy, but he was not amused. Then they told
me he came from Virginia, which probably explains why he was
not amused.

This all happened downstate, on an evening before the party
would leave to hunt deer. We made quite a group. Gus Garcelon, my dentist friend and firearms buff, was a director of the
National Rifle Association, and the summer before had invited
some of the staff in Washington to come up to Maine to get their
deer. They had now arrived, and Colonel Lee was one of them.
Bright and early tomorrow we would leave in several automobiles for Daaquam, Canada, on the Quebec border. There we
would pass the chain, cross the St. John River, pass Clayton
Lake, and continue to Umsaskis Lake, on the Allagash River,
where we would use the fish and game wardens' camp. It's a
good camp with conveniences, proper and ample for the digni-
taries we were entertaining. Besides the NRA folks, Gus had
recruited a number of us rugged natives to guide, entertain, and
nursemaid the guests.

Gus (we call him Dr. Gus when formal) had made all the
arrangements, and he had the necessary passes from Interna-

tional Paper that would get us through the Daaquam chain. He also had complimentary hunting licenses for the NRA boys. Off we took and away we went, but Colonel John Lee, driving alone, planned to pause at L. L. Bean's for some item he needed, and I, also driving alone, meant to stop in Bingham for a few minutes to see an old friend. This means that everybody went through the chain together except Colonel Lee and Admiral Gould—and we came along later.

Colonel Lee arrived at the chain first. The geography is rather remote there. On the northwestern boundary of Maine, somewhat following the St. John River, population is slim. The few towns on the Canadian side—Ste. Aurélie, St. Juste, Daaquam, Estcourt—are little more than access to Maine. As they say, you can't get there from here, and so must arrive through Canada. Daaquam has a store and a sort of hotel. A daytime-only Canadian customs station sits on that side of the chain, and the man who raises and lowers the chain for traffic has his camp. Next is the United States customs station, limited hours only, a game warden's house, and miles upon endless miles of trees. And here, at the jumping-off place for nowhere, was Colonel John Lee from Virginia trying to get through the IP chain without a pass. *On ne passe pas.* For at least an hour he had been shouting at poor Raoul Benoit, the keeper of the chain, who labors under strict orders about passes and who is easily able to forget his English and merely shake his head in French. I had known Raoul for many years, but I would never have expected to pass his chain without that slip of paper signed by Ben Pike. Which, of course, I had.

As I arrived, there was this automobile with a Virginia license tag drawn up in mid-road, driver's door open, and Colonel Lee waving his arms and shouting at Raoul over the chain. The manner in which Raoul spread his hands and shook his head was enough to tip me off. I played along.

"Bonjour, mon vieux!" I called. "Ça va?"

"Ah, oui, bonjou', bonjou', bonjou'! Toujours pareil, twee?"

"Paw peer," I said, which is Canuck for *pas pire,* and I added,

"Qu'as-tu là?" I nodded towards Colonel John Lee, and now Colonel John Lee turned and saw me.

"Wow!" he said. "Am I ever glad to see *you!*"

"Excuse me, sir," I rejoined with magnificent dignity, "I believe you have the advantage of me!"

Then I said to Raoul, "Ton épouse se porte bien?" He said there was no change, and I said, "Dis mille choses de ma parte," and John Lee jumped up and down and screamed. Today, he would remain composed, because today he has several visits to Maine behind him. Then, he was truly from away. I told Raoul in the patois of the region that Colonel John Lee was all right, that he was included on the Garcelon pass, and that after a short time he should be permitted to go through the chain and join the merry group at Umsaskis Lake. Raoul waved his arms and shook his head to convey that he didn't understand a word I said, and I drove out around Colonel John Lee's automobile to be passed through the chain. Raoul jerked the chain up again so it just barely cleared my tailpipe.

I had been in camp long enough to get my plunder stowed and the bedroll unfurled, and Colonel Lee arrived. It was just about three-quarters of an hour before he said anything, and then to the party as a whole he shouted, "For two solid hours that goddam Frenchman didn't know one word of God's English—and when he let me through do you know what he said?"

"What did he say?" asked Gus.

Colonel Lee looked all around.

He spoke. "He said quite a good deal, all in all. He spoke real schoolteacher English, and he said, 'Welcome to the North Woods, Colonel—enjoy your week and I'll see you on the way out.' That's what the bugger said!"

Then Colonel John Lee said, "What the hell kind of a put-on is *that* supposed to be?"

Gus said, "Welcome to the North Woods, Colonel Lee."

EIGHT

A very first State-o'-Maine no'theast rainstorm is worth remembering, and I remember mine. That's because I was ten. I was ten when my father's affairs caused him to move from Medford, Massachusetts, back to his native Maine and he bought the big house on Maple Avenue in Freeport. Our little cottage home in the Glenwood section of Medford doesn't linger too much in my memory, but I know that it was not wired for electricity. Things in the city are supposed to be better than that. Mother cleaned and filled her kerosene lamps every morning. She did have a gas range to cook on, and a meter down cellar that took quarters. Sometimes with a cake half baked she'd have to go down and shove in a quarter. And I remember that when I told my Medford friends that we were going to move to Maine, they seemed to pity me. Away up there! Leaving the advantages of civilization and culture was unthinkable. So when we arrived in retarded Freeport and moved into our new home, we had electric lights!

Except in my room. Mine was up attic. The west end of that attic was open, a considerable space with rafters and roof boards exposed, and a loose floor. A typical catchall. But on the east end, just at the head of the narrow, steep stairway, laths and plaster had been put up and a room finished off. There was a door to close out the open end of the attic and window in the gable that didn't raise or lower. I had to lift it out frame and all when I wanted air. Several years would go by before an electrician ran a line up to my room. Neither had I heat, but that was a relative thing. The coal-burning furnace down cellar did a reluctant job through the first-floor registers, and was always very quiet about the upstairs. Had there been a pipe to my room, I probably would have been no better off. By closing one register we could direct heat to others, and if somebody wanted a bath the rest of the house would cool down accordingly. My small room, sloping with the roof, had rosebud wallpaper, my three-quarter bed, my bureau, my chair, and—as time ran along—the accumulations of an active boyhood. It also had a view of the village and first crack at every sunrise. When I finished my school lessons and went up to bed, everything downstairs ceased to be, and I was alone in my altitude. It was May when we moved in.

The first night, I heard some new noises. I heard my first whippoorwill. I lay there in bed, the soft spring night outside my window, and stared popeyed into the dark as the foolish thing went on and on like a phonograph with the needle stuck. Then he stopped, and then he commenced again. That night, too, I learned about train whistles. In Medford the little commuter things that ran from Medford Square to North Station didn't whistle that I ever heard, and now I was introduced to the main-line traffic of the Maine Central. The Maritime Express howled through Freeport just shy of midnight at reduced speed of eighty miles an hour. Freeport had eight grade crossings from the Hunter Road to Allen's Range, and the engineer blew two longs and two shorts for each. This amounted to holding the cord down, and the great chime whistle of the steam locomotive saluted Freeport, and me, in one extended blast. With whippoorwill and whistle, my first night in Maine was a dandy, and about the time I got to sleep the birdies began for daybreak. In Medford, we had pigeons and English sparrows. In Freeport we had neither pigeons nor English sparrows, but we had everything else. They chirped and tweeted from the first suspicion of dawn, the melodious twitters of the pretty ones in the foreground of a raucous squawking of crows in our back-yard spruces. I was up, and down, early that morning, and in the kitchen my mother asked if I'd slept well.

I had just about become accustomed to the midnight passage of the Down-East Howler, in the manner of all Freeporters, when the twenty-fourth of May arrived. The twenty-fourth of May is Victoria Day, a Canadian holiday, and pretty nigh every Canadian in Boston went home for the occasion. That night the Maritime Express ran in two sections. The first had barely cleared Allen's Range when the second hit the Hunter Road.

So I listened to the night sounds of Maine, and they included rain on the roof. My pillow was less than three feet under the shingles, and a soft, springtime shower would lull me. But a hell-ripper of a down-Maine no'theaster is something else again, and I still had that to come. The no'theaster follows a pattern. We will have a serene and beautiful day. Blue sky as blue as blue ever was, and not a cloud. Don't be misled—the old Mainers call that kind of a day a "breeder," and bad weather is on the make. If you watch, you will see the high sky begin to show faint streamers that foretell a "smearin' in." They spread and multiply, and soon you have a mackerel sky:

> Mare's-tails and mackerel sky,
> Never twenty-four hours dry.

A storm is on the way, and it will break on the next turn of tide. Air begins to move, the clouds thicken and become gray. And now comes a steady wind off the Gaspé, off the Baie de Chaleur, off the Grand Bank, and it begins to gust, and it begins to rain. A Maine no'theaster works backwards. It begins to rain in the southwest, and Boston and New York will have it before we do. But it builds up as it comes, and it larrups around for a day and a night, and it's a good time to be snug and secure. It's a good time to be in bed.

My first Maine no'theaster ripped great sheets of water against my attic window and rattled it. It beat on my shingles. The wind creaked the timbers of my roof. There was no whippoorwill that night that I knew about, and if the Halifax train tooted for the eight Freeport crossings, the wind outdid the whistle. I slept after a time, but I was aware even so of the weather. By daylight the storm was over. Maine no'theasters clear off the same way they start—in the southwest—and if they clear off properly the wind veers. That means it follows the sun, clockwise, and is said to "haul around." That night the wind hauled around, and the sun came up bright to bring into bloom the bower of my rosebud wallpaper. I took out my window, which had been left in against the wind and rain, and there was the State of Maine clean and beautiful. A pool of water in the driveway, and a pear tree had lost a limb. A bull robin was working the lawn, and the crows in the spruces seemed content. I went down my attic stairs into the house, and found my mother at the kitchen stove. She pushed the home-fries aside with a flipper and broke in an egg. Generally she'd ask if I'd slept well, but this time she didn't.

"Wasn't that a lulu?" she said.

I've seen many a down-Maine lulu since that one, and they come and they go. I never tire of them. That first one introduced me properly.

NINE

William Zorach was born in Lithuania in 1887, came to the United States as a child, and lived at Robinhood in Maine until his death in 1966. I know little about his earlier paintings, but after he turned to sculpture I came to know him and to admire his talent. Look at his statue of Benjamin Franklin at the post office in Washington, D.C. We went on a party together one time, and I would like to repeat it.

The whole story is unlikely. It began at the annual Kellogg Day exercises of the Harpswell Garden Club. The summer colony comes to be seen, and anybody in Maine who can tell a verb from an osprey is invited to join the literary capers to do homage to the Congregational parson Elijah Kellogg, whose twenty-nine novels for children are happily forgotten. This event takes place by the old Harpswell meetinghouse, and across the way is the handsome church where Elijah Kellogg preached. Mine was a new name on the roster of Maine hacks that year, and I felt honored at the invitation to speak.

Besides his stories, Elijah Kellogg gave us a couple of speaking-contest declamations that are classics and in Maine are standbys. These were pieces written on purpose to be delivered by schoolboys, and so long as those oratorical contests were prevalent, almost any Maine lad could repeat them. One, the lesser, was "Regulus to the Carthaginians," which began, "The golden beams of the rising sun had gilded the lofty domes of Carthage. . . ." The better known was "Spartacus to the Gladiators." Since 1846, when Kellogg wrote the thing, Spartacus had been on the program of all regular and well-conducted declamation contests. I knew it. So when I rose to speak at the Elijah Kellogg exercises I easily began with:

> It had been a day of triumph in Capua. Lentulus, returning with victorious eagles, had amused the populace with

the sports of the amphitheatre to an extent hitherto unknown even in that luxurious city. The shouts of revelry had died away; the roar of the lion had ceased; the last loiterer had retired from the banquet; and the lights in the palace of the victor were extinguished.

I saw lips moving in the audience, as people joined in my recitation. I stopped after putting out the palace lights, completed my remarks, and the next speaker on the program was William Zorach, the sculptor. His presence certainly enhanced the program, but as he was in no way a writer I wondered why he was participating in a literary occasion. He said that he had an idea for a book, and that if he ever found the time to write a book, this was what it would be about. . . . His wit was good and he was well received and well applauded. He did say, as he began, that he, too, had memorized "Spartacus to the Gladiators," but would refrain from proving it. After the program I was standing talking with Zorach, and we were joined by a pleasant enough man who introduced himself as Peter Sammartino, chancellor of Fairleigh Dickinson University at Rutherford, New Jersey. He, too, had memorized "Spartacus to the Gladiators" as a boy.

Then he wondered if we, Zorach and I, with our wives, would care to come to his cottage at Prince Point in Yarmouth some evening soon to take supper and pass a few hours in congenial discourse. He and Mrs. Sammartino would be honored. This came to pass, and the Zorachs and we were served delicious choice beefsteaks done carefully to perfection. And as to the congenial discourse, it turned out that Chancellor Sammartino would like to have us, Zorach and me, come to Rutherford, separately, and lecture before the student body. We assumed his hospitality was intended to further the chances of our doing this, but as nothing was said about remuneration we never pursued his desire. I never saw Mr. and Mrs. Sammartino again, and I suspect the Zorachs would give the same answer. That's beside the point, which is "Spartacus to the Gladiators."

As we sat on the Sammartino porch with cordials after the delicious meal, the summer twilight creeping over Casco Bay, Spartacus came into the conversation, and I said the piece had a special charm because I had never forgotten any of it. Many a piece I had memorized for speaking contests had faded. I once memorized "A Message to Garcia," by Elbert Hubbard, a considerable composition, and another time I memorized "The Man without a Country," by Edward Everett Hale. Neither stayed with me any length of time, but I could run through "Spartacus to the Gladiators" without a hitch. The Latinity of the composition, I suggested, perhaps gave it that special quality. To prove it, I shouted off over the water, "Let the carrion rot! There are no noble men but Romans."

Zorach, at this, looked a mite puzzled. He seemed as if he might be wondering where he'd heard *that* before. Then he nodded, and then he stood up, and then he said, "I think it's time for me to confess."

Whereupon he struck an oratorical pose, gestured slightly right of front, and began to recite.

He went through the entire declamation of "Spartacus to the Gladiators." Every word; never a hesitation. In Yiddish!

Zorach had never heard the English version.

And I had never heard the Yiddish, but I would admire to hear it again.

TEN

The Model T Ford for 1917 was the last of the primitives. Sophistication set in, and the 1918 Model T introduced demountable rims and the starter. The starter was properly called a "self-starter," and to be on the safe side the 1918 cars also had the usual crank. The demountable rim was prophetic of the demountable wheel, but was to remain standard for many years. Jacking my 1917 Model T, my first automobile, and taking off a flat tire with the steel tire irons we Mainers called "spuds," was something to do numerous times during any trip of, say, four or five miles or more. Then the inner tube would be laid out on the flat top of the front mudguard, the hole would be located, and a rubber patch cemented on. Let the cement dry, reinsert the tube, return tire to the wheel with spuds, and then pump up 30-×-3½ tire with hand pump. Let car off jack, and proceed. The 1918 Model T also had an improved lighting system, so the magneto didn't blow out the bulbs so often. I drove my 1917 Model T—still cranking by hand and still spudding flat tires—until 1928, when the Model A was introduced. I bought a Model A "coop" with rumble seat, and all things considered, the Model A may be the best of all the automobiles, then and now.

Many boyhood memories of that Model T flock to mind—it went through college with me—but for the next time around I would choose a certain regimental reunion of the Sixteenth Maine Volunteers. My grandfather Thomas enlisted on his eighteenth birthday, and was one of the hundred local boys who made up Company I of that Sixteenth. Company I was raised from our local neighborhood, the towns of Bowdoin, Webster, Lisbon, and Durham. On the first day of Gettysburg the Sixteenth Maine held its position and at dusk was recalled—the official history of the engagement says, ". . . if 27 officers and men can be called a regiment." Other engagements of that stupid war took their toll, but five of the boys in Company I came home to Bowdoin, Webster, Lisbon, Durham. The five lived into their eighties and were still near by to Gramps in the days of my Model T. All belonged to the GAR—Grand Army of the Republic. There were Gramps and his tentmate, Benjamin Franklin Farrar. Then there were Dan Small and George Frost, and I'm guessing the fifth was named Osgood. I disremember, and today I wouldn't know where to ask.

These five renewed their wartime experiences twice a year. On Decoration Day they marched in the exercises to place potted geraniums in the cemeteries in memory of "fallen comrades." And every August they'd go to the regimental reunion, which would be held somewhere in south-central Maine.

These five men, as far as the State of Maine went, became the last survivors of the "blanket brigade." The Sixteenth Maine was unified with two regiments from Massachusetts and two from Pennsylvania into a brigade, under one command, and moved southward towards the war. When mustered in, the Sixteenth Maine had gone by train to Fall River, Massachusetts, and then by boat to New Jersey. The rest of the way—heading eventually for Gettysburg, as it turned out—was on foot, march all day and bivouac at night. This brave intention didn't work out altogether well. The War Department, which absorbed a good deal of blame overall in that war, didn't keep up with this march. Supplies didn't arrive, and after a time supplies didn't get sent. The five regiments bogged down somewhere this side of Washington and as Caesar expressed it so long ago, "went into winter quarters." After that, the men ceased to exist and they became forgotten.

It's true. Time ran along, and so did the war, and here were five regiments in bivouac with no contact whatever with authority. The men foraged, lacking supplies by wagon, and my grandfather used to say, "You can make a stew from about everything." Their farm backgrounds and their knowledge of the woods gave these boys from Maine an advantage over the others, and it proved useful to know how to pluck a rooster and dress out a cow. Gramps told about the time he was out on what he always called a "skirmish," and he came upon one of the

Pennsylvania officers who had just dispatched a farmer's milk cow with his pistol. Holding the bridle of his horse, the officer stood looking down at the carcass, and Gramps guessed the truth. He had a good piece of beef, but he didn't know what to do next.

My grandfather's prowess at the stew kettle had won him a promotion to sergeant, so he now approached the officer, presented his compliments, and offered to dress out the beast. Gramps told me, "I said I'd cut the thing up for the head." So he skinned out the cow and carved her, and he would say, ". . . and I contrived to bring the head away so most of the forequarters came with it." Company I of the Sixteenth Maine Volunteers dined well for several days. It paid to be a farm boy from Maine.

In time the plight of these forgotten soldiers was incredible. Their tents fell apart, and their uniforms rotted off their bodies. The War Department had simply lost them. And when, after the red tape and the bureaucratic folly, the five regiments came back into the record, and somebody remembered, an officer came to "review the troops." His report said the men of the Sixteenth Maine were "the poorest soldiers and the best scavengers in the Union Army." The historian of the Sixteenth Maine, Major A. R. Small, wrote about that bleak exposure: ". . . through storms of sleet and snow; without shelter, without overcoats, shoeless, hatless, and hundreds with not so much as a flannel blouse, many without blankets; and through all that we were jeered and insulted and called the 'blanket brigade.' "

The reviewing officer's report was unfair; another officer who came to see the misery of the blanket brigade said that while the War Department was asleep, "God has been making heroes." When the Sixteenth finally got to Gettysburg its performance left nothing to be desired. Grandfather told many things about that first day by Little Round Top, and he made light of some of them, but he would shudder so that I, a boy on his knee, could feel it when he said that he fired his Springfield musket sixteen times that day "—and every time I saw my man."

So there was much to hold these five surviving "comrades"

close, and in 1926 I drove all five of them over to the city of Gardiner for the annual reunion. Grandfather and Frank Farrar took the front seat with me, and the back seat held the rest. They wore their Grand Army uniforms, and one of them—I forget which—carried the *Boston Post* Gold-Headed Cane, the traditional New England privilege of the oldest man in town. My Model T Ford rose to the occasion. We had no flat tire, going or coming. She purred. The reunion was held at the Wadsworth home, halfway up the hill on Brunswick Avenue. Corporal Charles O. Wadsworth had been wounded in June of '62, and lingering effects had him now in a wheelchair. Otherwise his health was good, and his mind was sharp. These reunions were not limited to the old soldiers; the regimental association included friends and relatives, so women and children and nonsoldiers were there. It made a considerable group, and the Wadsworth home was filled.

During the program, which ran largely to reminiscences, his daughter wheeled Corporal Wadsworth forward, and he was in the center of the living room. He was a fine-looking gentleman, heavy-set, and he had a clear, deep voice when he spoke. "Comrades," he said, "do you remember our flag?"

I suppose the active members of the Sixteenth Maine had heard this recitation many times. To me, it was new. Grandfather never told me about the flag. Corporal Wadsworth spoke of a battle in the Wilderness Campaign that was going badly for the Yanks, and it was clear the day was lost. The Color-bearer wasn't about to let the standard fall into the hands of the Rebels, so he tore the flag into bits and handed a rag to each soldier within reach. The soldiers tucked the remnants into their uniforms, the battle progressed, and here we were in 1926 in Gardiner, Maine, recalling that day. Corporal Wadsworth paused properly, looked about at his comrades, and then reached a hand inside his GAR jacket. Out came a fragment of red cloth—Mainers call such bits "striddles"—and Corporal Wadsworth held it aloft and gave it a twitch.

The comrades cheered. There wasn't, as the saying goes, a dry eye in the house.

As we rode home in my Model T, Frank Farrar said, "That Wadsworth done a good job. Quite a man, quite a man."

My grandfather nodded, and then he said, "He was Company B—but a good man."

ELEVEN

Two Different People

The wild man of Borneo,
And Henry David Thoreo.

When I asked Flats Jackson and his comely Giselle if they
would canoe down the Allagash River with us, there
was more on my mind than his free services as the best riverman
in Maine. For one thing, as no man plays cribbage with his wife
as partner, so does no sensible person put his own wife in the
bow of his canoe. Let Flats paddle mine, and I'll have Giselle.
But that's not really the point; Danny O'Brien, then executive
editor of the *Boston Sunday Globe,* had asked me to do a series of
full-page stories on the Allagash, saying he had in mind a pres-
ent-day version of the old Henry David Thoreau stuff. He said
"stuff." Which is not all that bad, because Del Bates, who spent
a lifetime as lumber-camp clerk in the Thoreau region, once said,
"He got mixed up—mostly didn't know where the hell-ee-was."
Thoreau had come into focus at that time because Secretary of
the Interior Udall was plumping for a national park for the Allagash River, and Thoreau offered some useful quotations for the
brochures. And, while Thoreau comes to mind as a fine tub
thumper for the Allagash, the truth is that he didn't know much
about it. He came down Allagash Stream, and then did most of
his roughing it on the East Branch of the Penobscot. Look it up.

But the Allagash was in the news, and while the preservationists were going to "preserve" it, those of us who knew something about the Allagash and the Maine woods could only ask,
"Who do you think has preserved it so far?" Udall, you see, was
honking about this natural, unspoiled wilderness, whereas the
region had been logged off many times and was kept working
as a recurring tree farm by the private interests that Udall and

his like deplored. In 1966 the thing came to a head when the Maine State Legislature enacted the Allagash Wilderness Waterway into a perpetual preserve—partly to get Udall off our backs, and partly because state supervision was wiser than federal. Today the river is regulated so it's not much fun to canoe it, and the company foresters who kept an eye on the forests have been lost to our best uses. But before 1966, with the matter moot, Danny wanted to tell his readers what that country was like. Right up the middle of the state, through to the Canadian line— I suggested two weeks, and I made arrangements for Malcolm Maheu, the flying game warden, to pick up my stories and my film. Who better to nursemaid me on this errand than good old Flats? His woodswisdom was one thing, but I was also thinking about his infinite capacity to come up with things to write about. Where Flats is, things happen. Then, my wife and Giselle were compatible.

There had been, just before our junket, a "study" made by a team of—you guessed it—"experts," and it was pretty much a snide job. Some foundation had put up the money, and these professional grant-getters had produced just what Udall had wanted. I recall a photograph that showed the ravages of timberland by the callous butchers of the vested interests—that sort of thing. It was meant to make people say, "Well—it's time we did something about *this!*" Actually, the picture showed blowdowns after a windstorm in the Haymock Pond area, and the survey was blaming God's carelessness on the innocent foresters. Also, these experts didn't say a thing about the mosquitoes and black flies. All the recreational potentials were emphasized, but not a mention of black flies. How would anybody become an expert on the Allagash River and not know about black flies? Austin Wilkins, who was then our state forestry commissioner, explained that; he said none of the experts on the Allagash had ever gone down the Allagash.

So as this thing went on, Danny O'Brien's assignment really offered me one last chance to go down that beautiful watershed before it was lost forever to those of us who loved it. And when

Flats and Giselle agreed to go, I made the arrangements. Harry Sanders, a veteran at outfitting wilderness trips, packed our supplies, and provided canoes and tents. We found friends who would drive us to Telos Landing—the take-off—and meet us two weeks later at Allagash Plantation. And I built a special wangan box—*wangan* being an Indian word for all gear and groceries—which was tall enough inside the cover to accommodate a bottle. This was our liquor locker, and into it I put more than enough—enough not only for our social needs, but for our medicinal and mechanical requirements. Flats was a notorious advocate of bourbon whiskey, so I included bourbon whiskey.

In Greenville we picked up the things from Sanders, and we went along up over Rip Dam, through the Park, and came to Telos Lake. We said farewell to our friends and they drove away. Ahead of us were two weeks, the long mileage of the Allagash Waterway. We packed the canoes and went across Telos Lake to a campground on the far shore. We set up the tents, arranged the groceries, repaired the stone fireplace, lit our fire, and laid out our plans for the first supper of the trip. "Cocktail time!" yelled Flats, and he pounded on a frypan with a stick. I opened the liquor locker, arranged suitable containers, and poured Flats a hooker of his favorite bourbon.

"What's this?" said Flats.

"Bourbon," I said.

"Bourbon!" said Flats.

"Eyah."

"Migod, I ain't took a taste of bourbon for two years."

"What else would you like?"

"Gin!"

"We don't got any gin."

"Well, I sure as hell don't want any bourbon. Makes me puke. Can't touch the stuff."

Flats stood around and sulked. He kept thanking me for taking such good care of his wants. "Always thought you were my friend," he kept saying. There was still daylight to go when he blew up his air mattress and took it into the tent. We played a nightcap game of cribbage three-handed, and Flats explained, "Only play cribbage with my friends." At breakfast he was sullen and morose, if those two feeble words can convey what he was. Grunted at us. "Miserable night," he said, "haunted by fiends with bourbon whiskey."

That day, after breaking camp, we paddled twenty-two miles—up Telos, through Round Pond, into Chamberlain Lake, and to Lock Dam. It was a beautiful day, calm and bright, and by turning to look back we could see majestic Mount Katahdin. Flats insisted it hurt his eyes. That night we had an easterly wind, and it rained hard before morning. On the next morning we carried over to Eagle Lake, and began the true descent of the Allagash River, coming in the late afternoon to The Tramway, the site of the old log-hauling system that took Allagash timber over the mountain into the West Branch flowage. Plenty here for pictures and story, and I left my copy and my films for the game warden to pick up. There's a forestry-service station at The Tramway, and the warden then was named Emerson. I gave him twenty dollars and said, "Tell Malcolm to bring me in some gin next passage."

"Uh-uh!"

"What does that mean?"

"No can do."

"Tab-booze?" I said.

"Right! They'll fly about anything else, but no liquor. The State House would ground him if they found a bottle aboard."

"Hm-m-m . . ." The long-handled hm-m-m of a pensive moment.

"Tell you what," I said. "We need some tea bags. Have Malcolm fly me in a hundred tea bags."

"*That,*" said Emerson, "I can arrange."

So we moved along. We paused to fish Russell Brook, without much luck, but at Soper Brook we hit them just right. We brought twenty-eight handsome brook trout to the Ziggler Campground on Eagle Lake, just right for a chowder. Flats did help to bone them, but he kept making nasty little comments about how a spoonful of bourbon gives a chowder that certain zing, but how he'd much admire to have a zing or two himself of gin. Things like that. During the evening a fellow came up the lake with an outboard on his canoe and paused just offshore to call, "Gould here?"

"Right here," I yelled.

He said, "Your tea bags are down at Heron Lake."

"Thank you."

The next morning another canoe party paused to tell us the tea bags had been picked up and carried back to The Tramway.

"Pass the word to have 'em taken back down river," I said. "We're not going back to The Tramway."

So we got to the lunchground at Heron Lake and found a note that our tea bags were at Churchill Depot. At Churchill Depot, where a number of buildings of a 1930s lumber camp still stand, we found material enough to write about and to take pictures of to keep us two days, but we found no tea bags. And Flats Jackson was now the most vicious person in the world. Snapping at everybody, even people we met that he didn't know, and nothing pleased him. "Good morning, good morning!" I'd chirp on appearing from my tent, and Flats would say, "Sez you!" A party of Boy Scouts came down and paused before tackling the Chase Rapids, and the scoutmaster asked for me. "The Tramway sent your tea bags ahead to Umsaskis Lake!" he said.

After another day we came to Umsaskis Lake. Below the several exciting miles of the celebrated Chase Rapids, we lazied along in quieter water, and came to camp on a sandy beach on the east shore of Umsaskis. We chose that spot because there would be a breeze to help with black flies, and in the evening as we sat waiting for bedtime a herd of eleven deer came out to frolic on the beach for our amusement. They trotted up and down like a horse race. And as darkness fell, we saw the light of the forestry warden's camp over on the far shore.

The next morning we would pass out of Umsaskis Lake under the Bayley Bridge that is known as Hannibal's Crossing, negotiate the meanders of The Thoroughfare, and come into Long

Lake. We would camp at Long Lake Dam, a spectacular relic of long-log operations, where millions of board feet of timber were sluiced through every spring for the Allagash Drive. Flats, with my wife, pushed off, and Giselle settled into my bow to decorate my outlook. "Before we catch up," I said, "let's paddle across and see if the forest warden knows anything about our tea bags."

A Whistler's Mother lady sat on the screened porch of the camp, rocking chair active, and she watched us come across and arrive. We walked up from the float. There are never any strangers in the woods. And scarcely any news. A man can go into a city and hide away, but not into the woods. Somebody does something, everybody knows. How? Well, in the woods fashion. "You must be Gould," said the lady.

"That's right, and this is Mrs. Jackson."

"I surmised as much," she said. "I saw him and your wife pass the bridge just now." She gestured at binoculars at her elbow.

"Thought we'd stop and pass the time of day," said Giselle.

"Good you did," said she. "I've got your tea bags."

She went into the camp and came out with a cardboard box. It was bent closed, but it wasn't tied. When she took her hand off the top, the thing flew open so anybody could look in. She pressed the flaps down again, and forced them to stay shut. "Been here since yestiddy noon," she said.

So, soon we followed along down The Thoroughfare, and we caught up just about where Long Lake begins. We had a following breeze, so we pretty much drifted the length of the lake. We came to Long Lake Dam early in the afternoon—earlier than our usual time for planning camp. I gave the cardboard box to Flats and told him to take good care of it. "What's this?" he asked.

"Tea bags."

"*Tea bags!* You and your G.D. funnybone!" He lifted the cover and looked in.

Giselle and I already knew what was in there. Beautiful old Malcolm, the pilot, had brought us in a hundred tea bags—and two quart bottles of gin.

Given the chance on another time around, I would like to sit on a driftwood log, as I did that day at Long Lake Dam, and watch Flats, after the drought, resume his customary happy ways. I didn't lift a finger. He brought the wangan from the canoes, rigged the tarp, and set the provisions under cover. He pitched the tents. He drew the canoes up, and then carried them, Indian fashion, around the dam so they'd be ready for the morning start. He swung an ax around for a few minutes and piled up enough firewood for a week. He went below the old sluiceway of the dam and in a matter of minutes came back with trout for all. He skirted the old campsite, now overgrown, found the well, and came back with a pailful—we'd been using river water, but tonight we had clear, cold, proper, water. The three of us, with nothing to do, sat and watched. Flats made witticisms and pleasantries, and paused to relate comical things that had just occurred to him. He made supper all by himself—the first time on the trip—and he brought the plates to us where we sat. During all this—Flats had a beautiful tenor voice—he sang "You Tell Me Your Dream" 384 times.

After supper he washed the dishes, but I insisted on wiping, and we did "You Tell Me Your Dream" a few more times. The light was fading when he blew up the mattresses. "Tell you how pleased I am," he said, "I'm going to blow up all of them!" He did. He took out his teeth, insisting he could blow better that way, and as the teeth lay there in the twilight smiling up at us, he filled all the mattresses and carried them into the tents to be placed nicely under the bedrolls.

"There," he said, and after a goodnight touch of gin, not very much, he turned in. We heard him humming "Your Dream" for a few minutes, and then he began to snore.

In the morning he tumbled out at dawn, sloshed around in the pond, wiped generously with the towel, and started breakfast. We were glad to have Flats back. "First good night's sleep I've had," he said. "Thank God for tea bags."

We broke camp, and last of all Flats let the air out of the mattresses and folded them into the canoes. Just before we headed down, looking forward to Allagash Falls, I went back to our campground for one last check. We hadn't forgotten anything, hadn't left anything. Except that Flats had blown up the mattresses, nobody would ever know that we'd been there. The telltale was in the air—Long Lake Dam must have smelled of gin the rest of the summer.

TWELVE

Weddings hardly get to be a habit, but wedding anniver-
saries come with regularity. There was one of mine
(ours!) that was a bit different, and it would be fun to run it
through again to find if it would turn out the same. Al and I
missed a wonderful opportunity.

Al is not my wife. He is my friend, and with our wives we
were making the great Gaspé tour. It was October and late for
that trip. Most of the accommodations were buttoned up for the
winter, and there had already been cold weather. On October
22 we came to Rimouski, which is rather much the starting point
for the clockwise drive around the peninsula. Clockwise is right,
because then you are on the inside of the coastal curves; t'other
way and you are cliff-hanging. October 22 is my (our!) wedding
anniversary, and this was the only time that she didn't get her
roses. Al, who was driving, pulled in at a Rimouski shopping
mart so I could go looking for roses.

Rimouski, while far out, is not a small place. It has good stores,
And *rose*, like *taxi* and *Coca-Cola*, is a universal word. I applied
severally, and got *nons* and headshakes, and there were no roses
to be had in Rimouski. Nobody likes to see a record broken, and
I had been faithful with the roses. In a department store I found
a corner that offered house plants and, in season, flowers. But
flowers were not rightly in season in Rimouski in October, and
the best I could do was a sad stem of pompon chrysanthemums
that had probably been white when they were not attached to
the parent stem in some far-distant hothouse. Now, they were
off-white and crowding yellow, and not long for this world.
Without shame, the store took my money, which wasn't much,
and I carried my nosegay out to the automobile. "Happy anniversary!" I said. "Here are your roses, with love!" And we drove
on, because to be sure of an open motel we had to be in Mattan

by late afternoon. By that time my wife's roses were touching on the brown, very droopy, and not at all romantic. As we registered at the Motel Belle Plage she asked the clerk if he could find her a vase (easy enough, an English vase is a French *vase*), and when he brought one she arranged her "roses" carefully for taking to our room. The clerk looked as if he considered her care a bit overdone, but when she told him that these were really beautiful, long-stemmed, red roses, he drew back somewhat.

The Motel Belle Plage is about as good as you'll find on the Gaspé tour. It faces north onto the St. Lawrence River, and from a harbor basin in the foreground the ferries sail to Anticosti, Sept Isles, and St. Pierre. Seas can run heavy there, so the shore is always interesting. The management provides a flock of ducks to entertain guests. The rooms are fine, the dining room is excellent, and the staff is friendly. French helps, but is not required. The lounge below has a big fireplace, and a blaze was at work when we went down for preprandial encouragement. A blaze at Mattan in October makes sense. After an apéritif apiece we went up for lamb chops and then dallied at table over cordials. This was our anniversary party, so we did everything right. Then, because the ride had been long and tiring, the two women decided to call it quits, and after Al and I saw them to the rooms we descended again to the lounge, purposing to take a nightcap and then retire. But the rest of that evening is the part I would like to try again, to see what would happen on another chance.

The cocktail waitress, a trim lass, had served the four of us earlier in some reserve, but now that the boys were alone she felt chummy. She greeted us in good Yankee English, whereas before supper she didn't know any English. "You sound as if you might be from New Bedford," I guessed.

"Nope. I'm Mattan, but I lived sixteen years in Fall River. Went down to Brockton first, and wound up in Fall River. You folks from Mass.?"

She fetched beers, and as she moved about her work she was chummy with others, and soon she began introducing folks. "These two are from Maine," she said to the couple across the way, and to us she said, "They're from Ohio."

Gemütlich is not a word that comes readily to mind on the South Shore of French Quebec, but that's what this amounted to. The Ohioans joined us, and before long, tables had been pushed together and everybody in the lounge made one happy company. It became one of those things where everybody buys a round, and our waitress was giving us every care. Then, the bartender, who had remained aloof from our merrymaking, shouted "Quatorze!" and our waitress disappeared.

She was back shortly and gave us her attention until the bartender, again, called "Quatorze!" After several quatorzes, with the consequent short absences of our waitress, I asked her what was going on up in room 14. "The judges," she said. "They play poker." And she left us again when the bartender called "Quatorze!" Whenever room 14 called down, she would take up the drinks. She explained that once a month the circuit-riding judges, four of them, come from Quebec City and hold assizes around the Gaspé, disposing of matters that have been saved up for them, and during their regular sessions in Mattan they stop at the Motel Belle Plage and pass the evenings with poker in room 14. Then our little party broke up, and Al and I, alone, were about to turn in. As we started from the lounge, a dapper young man with a small mustache came in, approached the bar, and said, "Nightcap, Alphonse!"

Alphonse reached for a glass.

Al, always outgoing and friendly, said, "That's not a bad idea—mind if we join you?"

So the three of us took stools, Alphonse provided, and it turned out our friend was one of the judges. "Too bad I didn't know you were here in the early evening," he said. "I'd have asked you to join us in fourteen. It's a small game; no great amount of money passes hands. Just our evening amusement on the circuit. Too bad."

We thought it was, indeed, too bad. On another time around? Well, wouldn't it be fun to say that on my wedding anniversary I played penny ante with the Superior Judicial Court of the Province of Quebec?

THIRTEEN

When I was growing up in Freeport, here in Maine, Pumping Station Brook was off limits. The town water supply came from there, and the public was required to keep a distance. Our health officer said the water wasn't fit to take a bath in, and referred to the source as "a dammed brook." It was so. Things went along easier in those days, and the water was allowed to stagnate in a pool that was meant to filter. Nobody knew about chlorine. A tub would have a mellow, coffeelike color, and at the kitchen tap the glassful drawn to refresh the customer suggested molding autumn leaves and the deep recesses of a swamp. Complaints about Freeport water were constant, and the company that owned the utility often responded from its Portland office that it hoped soon to give the matter some attention. There was, accordingly, little reason to restrict activity along that waterway, but swimming was totally forbidden and every ten feet there was a sign that said NO FISHING.

These signs proclaimed a monstrous untruth. The best fishing in the State of Maine was right there by the pumping station, where the water was rich in plankton and other ichthyological nutriments, so that in about three months fry would become beautiful brook trout that averaged a pound apiece. It was on a warm, late-May evening that my father, who was otherwise law-abiding and respectable, sneaked me through the puckerbrush to the water's edge and said, "Try there!" I was underage then and needed no fishing license. When I became of age I bought one from our town clerk, and it cost me twenty-five cents. It was to be good as long as I remained a bona fide resident of Maine, but the state has long since welched on that and never even offered to return my quarter. I still have that license, now in protective plastic, and once in a while I hand it to a warden who is "checking" me. An older warden will smile and pass it back, but the young ones never knew about those old lifer tickets, and it's fun to watch them look mine over. But I was underage on that memorable evening of my first trout hunt, and the trout didn't ask me about a license. They were snapping great circles out of the water, and they'd hit my hook before it got wet. Since Dad and I were trespassing willfully and poaching deliberately, there was no need to heed the bag limits, so we took home a good catch, which in Maine is a "nice mess of trout." It was two nights after that when the superintendent of the water works and two constables caught a neighbor of ours as he was fishing the same spot, and the law used him severely. One of the first laws of angling is to obey the regulations made and provided; another is to avoid being caught.

Making a first fishing foray like that happens to be something you can repeat. The next time around comes when, as a man, you take your own son to a brook. A generation apart, two moments become one, and there you are, both son and father. Thirty years after Pumping Station Brook, on another late and warm May evening, we were planting the sweet peas. It isn't everybody takes the time to lay sweet-pea seed in right, and that may be why fewer fathers take fewer sons to fewer brooks every May. I was instructing my laddie—spade deep and make a wide trench. Ladle in a healthy dose of cow manure. Soak the seeds a few hours in water, and then lay them in a row in the trench. Some say a sprinkle of dirt should cover the manure before the seeds are laid, but that isn't so. Sweet peas like to eat, and they start right in. Then cover the seeds with about an inch of dirt, press down, and wait for the sprout. Later, hoe the plants, but if they have their deep, wide, rich trench to start with, you've done things right. Pour some water in the trench in dry times. All this I explained, and as we spaded the trench I kept picking up the earthworms that appeared until I had quite a snatch of them in a can. "What are you going to do with them?" he asked.

"There is a reward that goes with planting sweet peas," I said. "It is in my mind to approach Perkins' Brook and dispose of these worms in an orderly manner."

Lacking a Pumping Station Brook for this second time around, I had scouted Perkins' Brook, and just above the Sleeper Farm I had found a beaver flowage. I would rather have a pair of beavers managing my wildlife affairs than all the biologists in the world, and here I could see that my faith had been heeded. The dam was fairly wide and quite high, so it made a pond of some size, but it was not going to be easy to fish. A lot of trees to get a line tangled. I guessed the dam was two–three seasons old, so the trout behind it should be respectable. When the average angler comes to a flowage of this kind, he usually passes it by as too hard to reach. It's worth the work. If you watch a while you will usually see a trout break water, and that tells you where the thread of the stream was and where the pool is now. Next, you need to find a way to get near enough to drop a fly or a worm. I didn't fish the dam the day I found it, but I located a shallow place where a short-legged boy could get to the splash I saw. No trees in the way, either. The situation offered the best chance I ever saw for beaver-pond fishing, so I felt my son was likely to do as well as I did at the pumping station.

Two evenings later we planted the sweet peas.

Memory prevails. You see, I wasn't really taking my boy to fish Perkins' Brook. My Dad was taking me again to poach the filter pool. All at once I was playing two parts—and if the first role was illegal, the second was all right. As My Dad, I led a boy to the beaver pond in stealth, cautioning him that trouts shy at vibrations and shadows. As My Son, I thought this made sense, whereas with Dad in his time it had made all the more sense— keep quiet so nobody'll know you're there! As My Son, I took seventeen trout that evening before twilight made us head for the road. My son didn't need a license at his age, either, and the count was legal at that time—two of us and a bag limit of ten apiece.

Because darkness came upon us, we didn't dress the trout at the brook. We did that in the sink back at the house, and Mommie to him admired his success just as Mommie to me had done before. It made a smart platter to put in the refrigerator—another "nice mess."

"We should plant sweet peas more often," he said.

FOURTEEN

When my father's uncle Levi was coasting along in his sixties, he used to josh about going up to play with his cousin Jimmie. This was James Edgecomb, and he was a cousin. Jimmie lived in the town of Industry, a few miles out of Farmington in Maine's Franklin County, on a farm that looked down off a ridge onto a lake. Uncle Levi did visit Cousin Jimmie now and then, but the word "play" was whimsey. They were not of an age, because of the way the generations overlapped, and while Uncle Levi was sixty-something, Cousin Jimmie was knocking on his centennial. When he did reach his hundredth birthday, everybody went up to Industry for the big party, and Cousin Jimmie himself had added a nice touch to the occasion.

On the morning, just at the edge of light, there had been a commotion in his pigpen. He hurried out from his bedroom and found a black bear. The pig was making quite a touse, and didn't like matters a little bit. So Cousin Jimmie, on his hundredth birthday, started things off by shooting a bear with the ancient Queen's Arm that his grandfather had carried in the Quebec campaign of 1759. The bear, dressed out, was hanging in an apple tree on the lawn when the family began to gather for the party, and he added a sporty décor to the celebration.

It was a long day's work to get from downstate to Cousin Jimmie's place on the hill. Trains ran from Brunswick to Lewiston, and from either place you could get to Crowley Junction and connect with the up-train to Leeds, Livermore, Jay, Wilton, and Farmington. But from our farm Uncle Levi would be carried by horse and buggy to Crowley. The ride to Farmington was interrupted every time the train came to anything with a screen door on it, and Uncle Levi always referred to the "triweekly service." You went up one week and tried to get back the next. There was some kind of stage from Farmington out to Allens

Mills, and Cousin Jimmie's horse and buggy would meet Uncle Levi there. The visit would last three or four days, and then Uncle Levi would try to get home.

Cousin Jimmie was a bachelor, but had provided himself with a family by taking "state children." Orphans and underprivileged children could be had from the state welfare department by responsible households willing to bestow some loving care and good groceries. Many a lucky state child has grown up in a good home as "one of the family," and over the years Cousin Jimmie had many boys and girls come and go. But as he grew older and he, in turn, needed loving care, his "family" was three state children who grew up and simply stayed on. One was Lydia Gifford, still remembered in Industry, who became Cousin Jimmie's heir and stayed on after he was gone. The second was a man, a cripple in his foot, and about Lydia's age. The third was Harold Spinney, younger than the other two, and still able to do some farm work after they were not. Harold is the one I would like to see again on another time around.

As time ran along (even Uncle Levi was gone), the little household up in Industry was on our family's mind. None was kin, but they'd been mighty good to Cousin Jimmie. Now and then my father would get a newsy letter from Lydia, and she always made out that everything was, as Mainers say, nicely. My father would remark that somebody ought to go up and make sure they were all right, and now and then somebody would. One fall Lydia wrote, and although she protested that all was well, Dad read between the lines and decided to attend. We made the excuse of a hunting trip, and the two of us went to Industry in my Model T. Lydia, informed that we were coming, wrote back that the spare room was ready. My father had his heirloom .40-65 Winchester, and I borrowed L. L. Bean's .35 rifle. We took aplenty to keep us warm, and stopped at the Mohican Market in Lewiston to round out our supplies. Dad dropped a lot of money there, intending that we should have plenty to eat on our trip, but meaning to leave the leftovers to embellish Lydia's larder. Lydia would never call on, and Lydia would not be happy to embrace charity, but food left over from a hunting trip would not go to waste. So Dad bought a lot he knew we'd never touch. And he bought two thick cuts of choice beefsteak—Mohican Market being famous in its time for the quality of its meats. Off we went, side curtains buttoned on the Model T, eager for a few days in the woods and pleased at our stratagem for helping the distressed. When we began driving up Lydia's hill, there was light snow on the ground—excellent for tracking game.

We drove into the dooryard just after dark, and parked the flivver under the apple tree where Cousin Jimmie had hung his bear. The three lingering wards of Cousin Jimmie greeted us, and we carried in our things. Lydia took a lamp and showed us to our room—clean and neat, but cold. The only fire in the house was in the kitchen range. We sorted the groceries. Lydia had the table set for five, and now that we were five she sprung her surprise. "We don't get much seafood up here," she said, "so we thought seein's we got special company, why don't we splurge?"

She paused, considering the impact, no doubt, and she added, "We're going to have a clam chowder!"

I never cared much for a clam chowder anyway, even at the coast, where clams came fresh. We could have one any time we wanted to take a rake and a hod and look at the time of low water. Up at Lydia's, a clam chowder came from a can, and she had opened two cans. I looked at Dad, whose face was inscrutable, and I thought about those steaks we had just set in the shed out of the kitchen heat. Dad seemed to meditate, and I was ready to shudder when he would say, "Oh, that will be nice!" He didn't say it.

"Lydia," he finally said, "John and I have clam chowders back home so often they don't really amount to a treat to us. Fact is, we had one last night." (A lie.)

"So we appreciate," he went on, "how much seafood means up here in the woods where you can't have it too often. Tell you what I suggest—you folks enjoy your chowder, and we won't eat any of it on you. I'll rummage amongst the groceries we brought, and find something for us. Something that won't be taking clam chowder away from you."

Dad and I had steaks, home-fries, onions, a dish of green peas. The other three went at their clam chowder with incredible gusto—it was green from the lackadaisical luster of canned clams, and heavy from the special evaporated milk the canning factories use to hold their clams apart. Clams of that kind are hard to chew, and set heavily on the stomach. When the evening was over and Dad and I were putting on our mackinaws for going to bed, I said, "I couldn't have got any of that greasy, gray-green Limpopo chowder down."

"Neither me," said Dad.

The next morning Lydia had a superb breakfast ready for us after the manner of her own precinct. Lightly smoked farm ham, eggs over easy, hash-browns, and home-baked bread with home-churned butter. The coffee was good upland Maine coffee, boiled to superb perfection and fined with a raw egg. Cream for it. We were now free to tuck our sandwiches in our pockets and fare forth to seek the noble and tasty stag. "Would you mind if I came along?" asked Harold Spinney.

Of course not, and we really didn't. We thought he'd make a good guide, keeping us in the more likely parts of the country, and three in a party is a proper number. Not at all!

"Good," says he, "but first you've got to run me over to West Mills to get me a license." We had a little trouble finding the town clerk, so our striking out was now delayed into the forenoon. When we got back to the house, Harold said, "Now, I'll only be a minute!" and he went inside.

He was gone a good deal more than a minute. He came out with the old Queen's Arm—the same gun Cousin Jimmie had used to shoot the bear so many years ago on his birthday. A collector's item of great price, the Queen's Arm was a military weapon of the French and Indian exercises—the soldiers who went to Louisbourg in 1745 had an issue of Queen's Arms, and so did those who returned in 1758. Later, in 1759, came the battle of Quebec, and from that occasion Cousin Jimmie's grand-father had brought the gun back to Industry. Since then it had been the farm firearm. Harold Spinney now loaded it with a ramrod, pouring powder from a horn and dropping in a ball, and after he had primed the pan he gently set the flint down with a studied release of the hammer. He fitted the ramrod in its place and said, "There!"

Hoping did no good. A thousand times that day I prayed a deer would face up to Harold so he could pop him off with the relic. My father later said that he did the same, and kept his eye on Harold at the expense of seeing any game himself. Harold walked carefully, so as not to jiggle the powder in the pan and lessen the chance of a flint flash. We hunted hard, as they say, but not for ourselves—we wanted to see the Queen's Arm go off.

We saw no deer that day. Just before dusk we came back to the house and Harold used the screw-end of the ramrod to draw his charge. The ball went back in the pouch; the powder went back in the horn; the Queen's Arm went back in the corner of the cold living room. I never saw it again.

The next morning Harold said it was too much work to carry that cannon all day, so he stayed behind. Dad and I hunted, but deer were not for us. We got some pa'tridge and a snowshoe rabbit. The next day we packed up and came home, leaving four boxes of groceries for Lydia. Do you suppose that on another time around Harold might see a deer?

FIFTEEN

Most of the regulations by which a Maine lobsterman pursues his trade derive from premises of conservation, their intent being to keep the fishing good for years to come. But one regulation does not—the one that forbids hauling traps in the nighttime. Pirating another man's traps is known as "touchin' up," and the penalties for touchin' up are severe. Severe not only in the statutes made and provided but in the swift retaliation, man to man, when gear is molested. Only a thief pulls a trap outside of daylight. But a man can board his boat in the dark, cruise to his fishing grounds, and be all ready to "garfft" his first pot-buoy when the sun breaks the horizon and drips great blobs of red back into the sea.

Friendship, on Muscongus Bay, claims some three hundred lobstering licenses and lands more lobsters in a year than any other port. Friendship, thus, is a working port, even though the harbor gets its share of the summer mahogany. Once a year the Friendship Sloop Society brings the historical gaff-rigged boats back for a three-day, home-town regatta, and clutters the bay, but lobst'rin' goes on even so and a yachtsman is not esteemed if he ties up at a wharf and interferes with business. The harbor comes to life a couple of hours before sunrise, when the lobster catchers arrive at the shore in their pickup trucks and assemble in groups to assess the weather. It was a pleasant May evening in 1969 that I, lately a highlander, was introduced to the esoterics of Friendship. Harold Jameson, a lobsterman, paused by my garden to compare notes on the progress of planting. We had moved from our farm to a salt-water dotage, and I was making do with a small plot after deserting my upland acres. I was amazed when Harold said, "Like to go haul tomorrow?"

I am not Friendship, and being another kind of Mainer I know that my chances are remote. To coastal people a highlander is

anybody who lives farther from tidewater than you do, and there
is no remedy. As a highlander, I can dwell in Friendship, I can
pay taxes in Friendship, I can make friends in Friendship, and I
can live out my time in Friendship. But when I go down to the
shore—which I shall never be able to pronounce "show-wer"—
somebody like Harold is going to look up in feigned surprise

and say, "Why, hello! You down for the sum-muh?" Now, by some miracle, I had somehow bridged the gulf, and here I was—being asked to go haul! I always knew well enough that should I broach the subject and ask Harold to take me to haul, he would be more than glad to take me—but that's not the way it's rightly done. I would never ask. I bandy with Harold, and if I get the first word in at the stow-wer I will ask if he wants to borry some more money to clean up his gross-ree bills. This evens out the down-for-the-summer insult, and we get along. Now, the last thing for me to do was appear eager. There are rules to go by.

"Tomorrow?" I said.

"Eyah. S'posed to be a calm morning."

This meant not only that the weather would suit but that I needn't have qualms about *mal der mer,* as highlanders are presumed to be queasy about that. "Oh," I said, "I dunno." Harold knew I would go. So did I.

In a few minutes I said, "About two?"

That would be 2:00 A.M., and along in May that's about right. Harold said, "About."

I came to the wharf from which Harold rows his skiff out to his boat on the mooring the merest seconds before two o'clock. The lights on the wharf are set to shine landwards, so I was blinded and couldn't see anything of the harbor. There was a true glassy-arse calm and not a sound. Not one of the Friendship boats had turned a motor. Harold's skiff was on the float; he hadn't gone out. Neither had Tom Delano and John Lash, by the same evidence. Then, from the lee of the bait house and from the darkness came the call I suppose I had been expecting. "Well, Mr. Gould—are you down for the sum-muh?"

The only time that anybody in Maine ever seriously uses "mister," man to man, is in town meeting to address "Mr. Moderator!" Harold's jolly haw-haw at his own good humor was helped by Tom and John, and I joined the three with my back against the bait house, my eyes toward the darkness over the harbor. They were not just standing there. They were performing the daily predawn ritual that assesses the outlook for the day. To haul or not to haul? They (like all the lobstermen up and down the harbor) were looking out over the water they could not yet see, straining ears for telltale whispers of wind and tide. They feel things that tell them something. If there is a suggestion that it's "going to be some bumpy down there," they will not go out. They don't really *fear* dat debbil Sea—they respect it. But on this morning, as Harold had predicted, the weather pattern was getting an A plus, and the little group of four of us broke up when John Lash, without saying a word, left us, went to his skiff, pushed it into the water, and sculled out to his mooring. There was another splash as Tom Delano put in, and then a tholepin groan as his laboring oar took "holt." Harold and I went out to his *Blossom*.

Harold's custom, and I believe that of most Friendship lobster catchers, is to leave breakfast until the return to port. By starting down the bay before daylight, they can have their "gang" of traps attended by midforenoon, and some of them, anyway, can be home free by noon. That doesn't appeal to me, so I had brought a clamhod with sandwiches, Thermos, and lumber-camp molasses cookies. Harold had fueled and put his bait aboard the day before, so my clamhod was all we took aboard. I stowed it forward, and by that time motors were coming to life in the dark all up and down the harbor. As each purred and idled, lights came on. Harold now touched the button, and the engine down in *Blossom* responded smartly to the first rev and purred like a pussycat with a pan of new milk. Harold switched on his binnacle light, and then his radio. The thing squawked magnificently, as all the other fishermen were doing the same thing and all were too close to one another. The signals would level off as the boats moved down the bay and put distance between them. He turned down the gain so the radio was silent. When he got the mooring shifted over to his skiff and *Blossom* was free to swing with the tide, he snapped on his riding lamps, stood flat-footed before his wheel, and pushed the motor into gear. *Blossom*'s screw bit into the harbor, she leaped ahead in deliberate purpose, and we were off to haul!

Harold gave the radio a little power, and bit by bit we could "read" the fishermen as they gossiped and commented. Harold didn't speak to his radio, but he listened, and now and then he'd say, "That's George," or "That's Winfield." There is infinite charm in the way a transmitting Muscongus Bay lobsterman says "ov-vuh!" Around the black can and into the channel between Garrison and Long islands, past Morse's Island, and with us went the lights of other lobster boats heading, as we were, down towards McGee's, Franklin Light, and Mosquito Rock. Except for Monhegan Island, we would have nothing now between us and Spain. As for wind and tide, we might as well have been on Farrar's ice pond, and *Blossom* was like a billiard ball rolling on felt. We rounded an island point and picked up Franklin, and then Monhegan. And, of course, overhead the stars were brilliant in the special dark that comes before the light of morning. We were in the open ocean, far down, when the sun leaped adrip in the east. It was a burst, and the sea was incarnadine indeed. I was entranced by the spectacle, but shifted my eyes to Harold when *Blossom* eased off and the motor was slowed. In the darkness, before that burst of light, Harold had brought *Blossom* so one of his pink pot-buoys was exactly abeam at the first legal instant he could touch it! He garffted it, threw the warp over his "wench," and salt water spewed aboard with the line. The trap breached, Harold had it on his washboard, the lid was open, and he was reaching into the "bedroom" to see what he might have. Nimbly, quickly, he laid the "counters" in his box, hove the shorts and starfish overboard, rebaited, and allowed *Blossom* to come full circle. When she was over the place where the trap had been, Harold pushed it overboard, threw *Blossom* into high gear, and off we jogged to his next buoy.

Harold's colors for his buoys run to a kind of frivolous pink. Each fisherman had his own colors. Now, I could see a line of Harold's pink buoys stretching out ahead—a line as straight as a string. Buoys with other colors were in that area too, hundreds and thousands of them, but Harold's pink showed distinctly, and I wondered how he could make *Blossom* come around in circles to lay the line so straight. I was purely a guest, and without a lobstering license I couldn't touch any gear. I couldn't help Harold. So I stood to one side and watched, and before the sun had lost its daybreak red and the dawn colors had faded we had hauled that line of traps. As *Blossom* made her circle and the last trap of the line splashed from the washboard, I looked back—and there was Harold's line of pink buoys, just as straight now as when he had started to garfft! We moved to another part of the bay and found another line.

The number of traps a man will fish in a day is a "gang." The next day he will do another gang, and he'll return to his first gang after, maybe, three days. This was one of Harold's lesser gangs, about fifty traps, so we were finished early and I broke out the lunch. Breakfast. Then I rigged a mackerel lure and we fished on the way in. Harold had "hear'n tell" that mackerel had already appeared to the west'ard of Otter and Cranberry islands, so he brought *Blossom* back that way. We got a few, but not many, and Harold shook his head at his failure to "find" mackerel. "I dunno," he'd say.

Even with our run for mackerel, we were back at the wharf early. Harold had a good haul—attesting to all that I was never a Jonah—and after he refueled and filled his bait tubs for tomorrow he put *Blossom* on mooring and came ashore in his skiff. His day's work was done.

This was not my first experience in a lobster boat, but it was my first in Muscongus Bay and my first with Harold. After that I would pry myself from my highlander's bed to go again. On haulin' days he was there by the bait house with John and Tom, and I was always asked if I was down for the sum-muh.

John Lash, one of the considerable family of Friendship Lashes, later died, so this triumvirate now "goes two." Now and then, as we meet here and there in the village, Harold will say, "You can go haul with me anytime." Then he adds, "You know that!" Upon which I think of the great many people in this world who will never have a Friendship lobsterman say that to them. I doubt if any trip down with Harold will match up with that first one, when the sun came up by McGee's and the ocean was red. But maybe there'll be another time around—so I go with him again once in a while.

SIXTEEN

Forbidden Fruit was a certain flavor of chewing gum, pretty much licorice, and it could be had in only one place—from the mechanical gum machine in Mr. Derosier's store. Mr. Derosier was, I think, the only Frenchman in Freeport then, and his store was in a small building on the main street, between the feed store and Mrs. Fisher's boardinghouse. Upstairs, reached by an outside stairway, Mellie Collins had a barbershop and made fiddles. Mr. Derosier and Mr. Collins might have been straight out of Guy de Maupassant, and in my growing up I much admired them both. It would be fun to step into Mr. Derosier's store again, try my luck for some Forbidden Fruit, and then go up to let Mellie Collins cut my hair.

Freeport was plain WASP. Mr. Derosier knew some English but spoke just enough to conduct his business, and as nobody else in town knew any French he remained the odd one. He didn't have so full a stock as our other storekeepers, but he put his prices a cent or two lower, and you could trade there to advantage for certain things. He always wore a long shopkeeper's frock and a *habitant* cap. When you bought a few things he would tediously write the prices on a paper bag, add them in French, translate, and announce the English total. The gum machine was on the counter to the left, just inside the door, and in my time it was already an antique from away back. I have never seen but the one. Made of oak, the case stood about two feet tall, and in a glass window could be seen the sticks of gum that would come out, one by one, as customers put in cents. The machine would take only the gums provided by the company that provided the machine, and the several flavors were wrapped each in its own color, so what you saw in the little window was like a rainbow. Every so often would be a stick in a red wrapper—and that was Forbidden Fruit. Although the window was arranged so the gum could be seen, there was then a space and nobody had any way of knowing just which color would come out the slot. It was something like a slot machine, and the Forbidden Fruit amounted to the jackpot.

With a cent and a desire for chewing gum, one would approach the machine and insert the coin. Nothing happened for a second or two, and then there would be a click and some kind of governor would begin to whirr. Something like a clock getting ready to strike, except that there came no ding-ding. Just a whirr. This continued for just about a minute, then a stick of gum would come out, and after another four or five seconds of whirring the machine would click off and be silent. Once in a while the windup spring would quit halfway through the performance, whereupon Mr. Derosier would go behind the machine, open a door, insert a key, and wind it up. Mr. Derosier always did this without saying a word. If, when your stick came out, it had a red wrapper, you had won a prize. The prize was a five-stick package of Forbidden Fruit, which Mr. Derosier had in a box behind the counter. He would look at your red stick, hand you a five-stick package, and still say nothing. The Forbidden Fruit flavor, I have said, was pretty much licorice, but it was a loud kind of pretty much, and anybody chewing it advertised willy-nilly that he had been lucky at Mr. Derosier's. Some said it stunk.

Mellie—Mr. Melvin T. Collins—was almost dapper and affected a small and well-tailored mustache which he may have intended to identify him as a barber. He was a barber and he was a good one, but he was a man of many talents—one of them was making and repairing violins and another was playing them. His home was up the street, and in the parlor he built a small sloop every winter. His sloops were lovely and were always sold before they were finished, but to get them out of the parlor he would take down the side wall. He kept putting the side wall back every year so it would be easy to take down the next. When Mellie was at work on a sloop, his customers had to get their barbering in another shop. Since he made violins, Mellie always put a fiddlehead scroll on the trail boards of his sloops—the identification of ten or a dozen sloops at a time in South Free-port harbor. His haircuts cost twenty-five cents, and he used squeeze clippers—no power clippers then.

During the World War (now called World War I), sugar was on ration and hard to find. The Collins family were three—the son Clifford was my age—and none of them used sugar. But whenever sugar was available in a store, often no more than a half a pound at a time, Mellie would take as much as he could get and lay it by. In 1919, the Fourth of July, came the annual Merchants' Picnic, when the townspeople were shouted to a clambake and ball game by the storekeepers, a thank-you for the year's custom. There was always a table with a tank of strong coffee, cream, and sugar—but this year the wartime problems held over and not a storekeeper in town had any sugar. Mellie brought a piggin of sugar, enough to sweeten the whole community, and he passed it around to make himself the hero of the day.

So I'd get a stick of gum and go aloft for a haircut. My mother used to relate my attitudes to the length of my hair. When she thought I was particularly cussid she'd give me a quarter and tell me to go see Mellie. Mellie's several activities made his hours at any one of them erratic, so it was seldom anybody was ahead of me in the shop. Usually, Mellie would appear from his back room with a fiddle in hand, and the place smelled of varnish rather than pomade and lather. One time—which I certainly would like to experience again—began with his whirling the cloth about me and asking how my lessons were going, if Pa and Ma were keeping well, and if I meant to go out for baseball again. Just then Clifford, the son, struggled up the outside stairway with a bass fiddle that stood taller than he, fitted it carefully through the door into the shop, and said, "Pa, I think I've finally got that hard part!"

Mellie stepped back, and Clifford began to slap the bass fiddle like a man in a swamp fighting mosquitoes, and the barbershop resounded with a run of music that meant nothing to me at the time. When Clifford stopped, Mellie said, "I think you've got it!

Let's give it a try!'' He stepped into the back room and came out again with a violin. He tuned, tightened his bow, tapped his foot, said, "Ah-one, ah-two, ah-*three*," and off they went on a beautiful sweep of music that was truly through the looking glass—I watched them in the barber's mirror. With Mellie doing the tune-work, I now recognized Brahms, and they played on and on while I watched the mirror. The concert over, Clifford escorted his bass back down the stairs, while Mellie loosened his bow, laid the violin aside, and finished my haircut.

Some years after this, when Mr. Derosier was gone and his son Philip had taken over the store, I asked Phil if the gum machine was still around. It had been put out back, he said, when gum for it could no longer be had, and after some time had disappeared. Were it still about, he said, he would gladly give it to me. But I didn't need any material souvenir to make me remember Forbidden Fruit. I had hit the five-stick jackpot that day, and chewed Forbidden Fruit while I was getting Brahms with a haircut thrown in.

SEVENTEEN

The forty-acre wood lot that went with my grandfather's farm on Lisbon Ridge—the farm that was to become mine—was six miles away, to the east'ard beyond The Borough, in The Kingdom. Joshua's Kingdom to be exact, and Joshua was some kind of a nut that got religion in days long gone by and fancied himself a preacher. He'd stand on his piazza and preach, whether he'd anybody to listen or not, and in time that area of the town of Bowdoin came to be known as Joshua's Kingdom, so that when Joshua was forgotten people thought there was a biblical derivation. Not so; Joshua Coombs was crazier than a bedbug. One of the first stories I ever heard about him had to do with his seven-by-nine hog. He went into Bailey's Hardware Store and said his big hog had jumped through the barn window and had cleared the light of glass right out. "What's the size?" he was asked.

"Seven inches by nine inches." That's an unusual dimension for a hog, and for a generation or so it became the measurement of deficiencies. Anything that didn't amount to much reminded of Joshua's seven-by-nine hog. Long before Joshua that area had been the Crown grant to the Bowdoin family of Boston, and had been offered to anybody wanting to take up land in forty-acre lots at six dollars a lot. It was around 1790 that people began coming to The Kingdom and the lots were sold off under an arrangement known as "a bond for a deed." Evidently six dollars was a substantial price for those lots, because nobody seemed to have that much money. So a man would come, promising to pay in installments until he had reached six dollars, plus interest. He wouldn't get a deed to his lot until he had paid up. Meantime, he had merely the Bowdoin family's bond that a deed would be given. After a few years the lots belonged to a good many different people, and none of them had a deed yet. By the time the deeds were passed, there was no longer any need to recall the original surveyor's lines. Mr. Jones got a deed saying that his lot was bounded on the east by land of one Brown, on the south by Green, on the west by Gray, and on the north by O'Shaugnnessey. Simple enough, except that after a generation Messrs. Brown, Green, Gray, and O'Shaugnnessey, and even Mr. Jones, were long gone, and where was the lot? My grandfather picked up forty acres that were described in terms of adjacent owners, and for some fifty years he cut wood there and never knew where his land was. Neither did anybody else, and if people came to cut wood on him, so did he cut wood where he found a "good chance." The year I was ten in October, I went to that wood lot with Grandfather just before Christmas and had biscuits baked in a pail. It was my first introduction to his Civil War methods of camping out.

It was a cold morning after a light fall of snow. We had a good breakfast, and had packed the makings of dinner into a basket. He had Fan and Abel, his heavy horses, tied into the double logging sled, the traverse-runner rig Mainers called a two-sled, with hay and oats for them lashed to the rear bunk. Well bundled, we had the forward bunk, and as we jangled out of the dooryard the sun came up to shine in our faces. We rode into the sun all the way, through a shining world that nobody had used yet. There was one place that had an old owl perched on a limb over the road, and as we came along the owl flew ahead of us and perched again. We'd disturb him, and he'd fly again. The owl put the story into Grampie's head, so as we rode along he told me about the time his father had "shot" the goose.

His father had been riding in his buggy up in the other end of the town of Bowdoin, near Caesar's Pond, and a fox came out of the bushes on the pond side and started across the road with a fine goose in his mouth. It was a mouthful, so he held his head high, and he had no idea anybody with a horse and buggy would be around. Grampie's father, name of Jacob, let out a yell, and the fox, startled, dropped the goose. So Jacob brought a fat goose home to supper and he invented an explanation of this. He had been riding along, he told the family, when a flock of geese flew overhead. With great presence of mind he had stood up in the buggy and had slapped the leather seat cushion with the butt of his whip. This made a *crack!* like the sound of a gun, and this old honker on ahead heard it, thought he'd been shot, and fell to the ground dead.

We came into Joshua's Kingdom that day by an old county road that had been abandoned long ago, and Grampie pulled the team into a side road that ran along a brook. This was the place, and it was his reasonable presumption that somewhere in the vicinity, more or less, was his wood lot. On previous trips that fall he had cut and piled some wood by the brook, and today we would add to it and then bring the whole of it home. First we unhitched the horses, tied them to trees, and threw down hay for them. Grampie then kindled a fire against a big rock that showed the soot of previous fires. "Here's the way to build a fire," he said. He took off his hat and set it brim-up on the snow. Into it he laid small pieces of bark and dry twigs, forming a cluster about the size of a robin's nest. Now, he cleared snow away from the rock, and uncovered a small stack of dry wood sheltered by a piece of birch bark. (Before the day was out we made some new wood ready and left it covered for the next time.) All right! He took a wooden kitchen match from a small bottle, and he made me observe that the matches had gone into the bottle with their heads down. "If your fingers are wet, you won't dampen the heads," he said. He struck the match and applied it to the wad in his hat. He blew. The wad flared up, and he watched it for a few seconds. Inside his hat, the flame had taken, and no capricious breeze would foil it. And he dumped the burning wad out on the ground before it damaged his hat. Now he added dry wood, and it was amazing from first to last how little time had been spent at starting a fire. The rock began to reflect heat, and our basket of lunch was safe from freezing. Before he picked up his ax to go to work, he brought brook water and gave a little to each horse.

I wasn't expected to do any chopping, but I had an ax and I kept adding wood when our fire needed it. When the sun was high, Grandfather came to make dinner, and this is the part that could well be enjoyed again. He was now, once again, in his time, back in the Civil War, subsisting by wit in the open—a "scavenger" of the Union army. He wasn't obliged to "make do" this time with odd foods found and stolen, for we had the basket of things from the farm. Into the frypan went his bacon, cut in shreds, and after it tried out he threw in his diced onions. Instantly the clearing reeked of frying onions, and I wouldn't wonder if you can smell them in Joshua's Kingdom yet. The potatoes came next, and a cover was put on the pan to hold everything until, as he said, "osmosis sets in." We had pork chops and we had apple pie and he made a pot of tea. The biscuits were the thing, however, and he said this was how they made biscuits in the war.

When things were at their worst in the days of his blanket brigade, he was out on a skirmish and he came upon a slave cabin in a wood. Children scampered inside as he approached, and when he came to the door he got no response to his call. He went in and found a woman huddling with the children in a corner. It was dark inside, and they were black—it took a minute to accustom his eyes—and then he saw that they were terrified. He spoke soothingly, assured them he meant no harm to them, and he went outside to sit on the steps in the sun to see what happened. After a time the woman came out. They talked a while, and he took pains to explain that he meant no harm, that he was hungry and was looking for something to eat. Yankees, he promised, wouldn't hurt women and children. The woman sat silent for a spell, then got up and said, "Come."

He followed her into the house, where she stooped and lifted a trap door in the floor of the cabin. It was a small trap, by no means large enough for her, or any grown person, to pass. Now she took one of the children by the hand and lowered him into the hole. There was quite a space down there, because she reached him well down before she let go his hand. The boy passed up a bundle, and then he passed up another. She reached, lifted him from the hole, replaced the trap.

The first bundle was a ham, sewn into cloth and wrapped in heavy paper. The second was also wrapped in heavy paper, but under the paper was a cloth sack of flour. The flour, at one time or another, had been wet, and the outer portions had caked. But she told him the inside was good, and all he had to do was crack the shell. A Union commissary wagon had broken down "over yonder," she pointed, and before repairs could be made or another wagon could be brought, she and her children had carried away most of the provisions. Grandfather said he never knew what else she had stashed below, but that day he was happy with the ham and flour she donated to his purposes. He took them back to the bivouac, and . . . "Now," he said to me in the wood lot, "I'm going to show you how we made biscuits on a campfire."

He made them for me, he said, just as he made them for his company that evening from the soggy flour of the wet bag. Except that in the wood lot we had all the ingredients he would want for cream-tartar biscuits à la State of Maine. Even to a jar of fresh milk and dairy butter to assist them and to spread on when they were baked and hot. He got his dough right, then took the big pail and gave the horses another drink of water. They didn't finish all the water, so he hove the rest, and then turning the pail on its side he arranged his biscuits within. The pail was then set open end to the embers of our fire, and from the other side of the fire I could watch them puff, bake, and brown. If you have a pail you can bake biscuits.

What a feast that was! I rinsed off the dishes and packed things up for going home. He chopped another hour or so, and then we hitched in the horses and set the two-sled alongside the pile. We got almost all of the pile onto it, and we were well ahead of twilight when we had the team on the road home. But it was dark when we reached the house, and I had slept part of the way, leaning against Grandfather and under his arm.

I'm afraid I went to bed right away and can't say how we passed that evening, or even if we had any supper. But I've never forgotten how to bake biscuits in a pail, and I have in mind demonstrating the art to my grandsons when another time is propitious.

EIGHTEEN

When the computer moved in and specialization became a virtue, the Bert Coombses of this world waned. Maybe next time around, a destitute society will be more careful to perpetuate them, more sensitive about having them adorn the countryside. Bert Coombs was, as much as any man I ever knew, the living example of the Frenchman's definition of a gentleman—one who "prides himself on nothing." Bert had every talent, knew something about everything, was quiet, home-loving, public-spirited, hard-working, right-minded. I first knew Bert in his political, or public-spirited, capacity.

That forty-acre wood lot in Joshua's Kingdom was in the town of Bowdoin for tax purposes, and while it was true that nobody really knew exactly where it lay, the tax assessors of that sovereign civil division had no hesitation about levying the load. Bowdoin ran mostly to wood lots. My grandfather used to say the land in Bowdoin was so poor that a farmer had no chance. When a hearse went to a Bowdoin cemetery, he would say, a load of manure was always put in the grave under the casket. This was so a Bowdoin soul might have some chance of rising. Never did so many as a thousand ever populate Bowdoin's 28,000 acres, and to make a living a good many of them went to sea. So many ship captains came out of Bowdoin that in Liverpool people thought Bowdoin was America's principal city. Yes. So the year after Grandfather's wood lot was handed down, Bert Coombs came as tax collector of Bowdoin to collect from me. The tax on our forty acres was $2.28, which I paid. Bert gave me his receipt and retired into the quiet of Bowdoin. He had, to collect $2.28, made a round trip of over ten miles, and his commission on taxes collected was the standard 1 per cent. It stood to reason that Bert had some other means of support. The most valuable part of this transaction was that I came to know Bert Coombs.

Soon after I'd paid those taxes, something broke down on my mowing machine, and I was told, "Bert Coombs will fix that." So I learned that Bert was a blacksmith, and when I took my problem to him I found he was a farrier. Six or eight horses were tied up, he was shoeing another, and farmers stood around waiting their turn. The golden days of horseshoeing had passed, but as forge after forge was allowed to cool down Bert kept his hot, and enough farmers came from greater distances so that he had work enough. He remained for some time after that the only working smith in many miles. He promised to make my repair, ready for me on the next Tuesday, and I stood around an hour or so to watch him fit shoes. His shop had come down to Bert from his father, but smithing was on the way out and Bert knew that his sons would never ply that trade. Bert did odd jobs for me for some years.

As blacksmithing waned, Bert began to work on the newer household appliances. He was a Mr. Fix-it on anything from a leaky pan to an electric motor in need of rewinding. He came to know a lot about radios, beginning with the battery sets. These lingered longer in Bowdoin than they did elsewhere, because power lines didn't come to town right away. Bert didn't last into the age of television. He plumbed water systems, drilled wells, installed lightning rods, fixed milking machines, did automobile repairing. He was a carpenter, mason, and house painter, and did wallpapering. Because Bowdoin was late in getting electricity, he became an expert on small gasoline engines. He worked on home generators, and when electricity came by power line he went to wiring homes. He had a concrete mixer with gasoline power and did cement work. So, Bert kept himself occupied and picked up a penny now and then, here and there.

He dabbled in real estate, managed wood lots, and bought and sold firewood and pulpwood. His sawmill wasn't big, but it was busy. He sold insurance, and was president of the Merrymeeting Mutual. In his barn he had an antique shop and restored old furniture. He managed the baseball team—this was not a professional team, but organized just for fun, same as most

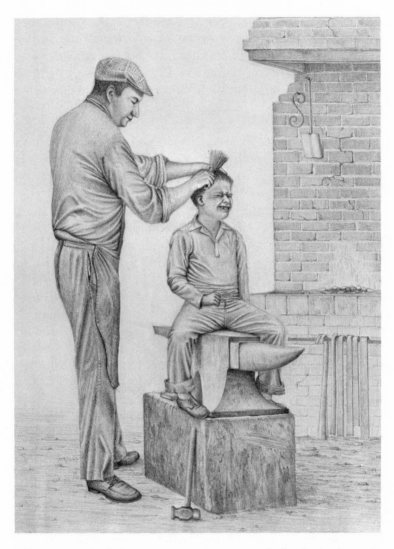

Maine towns had. I went to a game once, and after he had caught a few innings he went in and pitched. As a barber, he deserves a fuller description:

Bert and his wife used to take state children—waifs that needed a home. The state would pay board, but nobody ever got rich by this charity. Back when Bert was mostly the blacksmith, they had a lad of seven or eight years old who wasn't too swift— handsome little fellow with tow head, but not likely to win prizes in school. Bert took to the boy and the boy took to Bert—so much so that the minute school let out the boy would race to the blacksmith shop and Bert began referring to him as "my assistant." Come suppertime, he and Bert would walk home hand in hand. So one afternoon Bert noticed that this tyke's tow head had sprouted long, and he was in need of a haircut. There was no barber in Bowdoin—nearest one was ten miles away in Brunswick. "Sit up here and I'll clip you," said Bert.

Bert hoisted the boy up onto the anvil in the blacksmith shop, tied a grain bag around his neck, and cut his hair with the horse clippers that farriers used to trim tails and manes. The boy didn't look all that bad, at all. About anything Bert ever tried to do would come out right. Bert took away the grain bag and stood back to survey his work. Pretty good! He took down the horse- tail brush that was standard blacksmith-shop equipment, brushed the boy's neck, lifted him down from the anvil, and off they went for supper. The next day at school the boy proudly exhibited his new haircut and said Bert did it. So long as the boy stayed with the Coombses, and it was quite a few years, Bert barbered him when needed, always at the anvil.

Now, one afternoon Lester Murray came home late from his job, and his wife said, "You don't have too much time. Grange meeting!"

Lester had forgotten all about it. He was chairman of the pro- gram committee. He said, "Whyn't you remind me yestiddy? I need a haircut. I ain't got time now to get to Brumzick before the barbers close up." So just before Bert fastened the door on his blacksmith shop, in bounds Lester Murray to say, "Bert, I got Grange tonight and you got to cut my hair!"

Bert laughed and said he guessed not. He warn't no barber. Sure, he cut little Bojo's hair now and again, but that was differ- ent. But Lester wouldn't take no, and Bert got him to perch on the anvil. The grain bag was tied, Bert worked the horse clip- pers, and Lester got brushed with the horsetail. He tried to pay

Bert, but Bert wouldn't take a cent. But then Bert got to thinking things over, and he said, why not? It was a favor but it spared a trip to Brunswick, and Bert might just as well have the thirty cents that would else be spent out of town. So occasionally, but always as a favor, Bert barbered. He never set up a shop—people had to sit on the anvil and take their turn with the horses and the leaky pans. And one day Bert was fitting a shoe to a mare with ticklish feet, and he wasn't in what you'd call a receptive mood, and in walks a fellow dressed to the hilt, and he introduces himself as an inspector of tonsorial parlors for the state Department of Health and Welfare.

"You don't say!" says Bert.

"Yes, and I'm told you're barbering without a license."

"Gracious!" said Bert.

"I would like to inspect your shop," says the fellow.

"Be my guest," says Bert, and he pares a little on the mare.

"Where is it?"

"It surrounds you."

You can readily see why I hope the Bert Coombses are more prevalent on my next time around. When Bert told me about this, he said the state inspector was nowhere near so amused as he might have been. Bert toyed with him a time, and then told him pleasantly, man to man, how all this chanced to come about, and how his barbering wasn't really anything the state needed to jump up and down about. But the inspector said even if Bert got a license, his shop could never be approved. "Unsanitary," he said. Then Bert let him have it and told him to get out and stay out.

Bert told me, "I'd looked things up. The barbershop law made an exception of small towns, and Bowdoin didn't count. They warn't a thing he could do to me."

Bert chuckled as he told me this, reflected a minute, and then said, "But to be on the safe side, I called the governor that night. I'd been shoeing the governor's track horses for years, so I got him right away at the Blaine House. He laughed like to die, said he'd speak a word for me, and I never heard no more about the matter. I barbered when I'd a mind to and when anybody would let me, but I did send away and get a real barber's brush for wiping necks. I didn't like the idea of the horsetail too much myself."

Bert ran what I presume is the only real manufacturing plant Bowdoin ever had. He made spangle cloth in a shed to the rear of his smithy. Spangle cloth is glittery, and is used in circus and theatrical costumes. At the time, all spangle cloth came from Germany, where the secret of its manufacture kept it exclusive. Bert was reading about this in a magazine, and he thought about it a minute and decided there didn't have to be any secret. He put up the shed, made his machine, and set up a gasoline engine to run it. He found he could buy the glitter stuff by the barrel, all colors. Then he bought adhesive tape in rolls from Johnson & Johnson, the folks who make Band-aids and such. Big rolls, up to seventy-two inches wide. After a little experimenting, Bert was in business. He had a hot steampipe, and as the adhesive tape passed over it the stickiness was made just a bit more so. At this stage the specks of glitter fell and were evened out by a good shaking of the cloth. When the glitter was evenly distributed and the stickiness was cooled a mite, the product was just like cloth. He rolled it in bolts and sold it to the circuses by the mile. When Ringling Brothers & Barnum & Bailey came to Lewiston one summer, Bert went to look at his spangle cloth on the elephants, and also on the performers. Hollywood bought a lot.

I should add that Bert directed the church choir, sang bass, and had written some Sunday-school cantatas. He also played an alto horn, and had written a couple of marches that his band played on Memorial Day. Meantime, he would come every year and collect $2.28 taxes on our wood lot. We laughed about that because Bert, I, and the town of Bowdoin never knew exactly where that wood lot was. "If you want," Bert said one time, "I'll take my theodolite some pleasant day and we'll see if we can find a corner."

"You do surveying?"

"Some," said Bert.

NINETEEN

Great steamers, white and gold,
Go rolling down to Rio . . .

—Rudyard Kipling

No vessel, Rio bound, appeals to me. There is no magic there to my jaded experience. For I, when I was only six, sailed from Boston to Maine on the *Governor Cobb*. Rio, indeed! The *Governor Cobb*, too, was white, and memory adds the gold. The first thing I ever saw in the State of Maine was Seguin Light, through a porthole of the *Governor Cobb*. Seguin is the beacon at the entrance of Sagadahock Bay, the end of the Kennebec River, and an hour after I saw Seguin in the gray dawn, I stepped from the steam heat of a stateroom into the brisk, clean, cruel, bone-snapping, December air of a Maine morning that was, my grandfather said, four clapboards below zero. I was on the Eastern Steamship Wharf at Bath, Maine.

Back when the Republican party held the State o' Maine in its chubby palm, William T. Cobb of Rockland, Maine, had been a faithful altar boy in the devotions. When he was elected mayor of Rockland, everybody knew that he was merely going through the chairs and would one day be governor of Maine. It was in 1900 that a reporter said to him, "Tell me, Your Honor, do you plan to run for governor this year?"

"Oh, my goodness—no!" he answered. "It's not my turn!"

It became his turn in 1904, and he was elected. The next new white steamer of the down-east fleet was named in his honor, and Governor Cobb graced the dedication ceremonies in the usual way. The *Governor Cobb* was still paint fresh when my father took me from Boston to Maine to meet my grandfather for the first time. Dad was a railway postal clerk and worked from Boston to Bangor, so to him a ride on a train was workaday. Not only that, but the Eastern Steamship Line provided, in some ways, better service into Maine than did the railroad. We left Boston in the evening, had the comfort of a stateroom, and were on the wharf in Bath before breakfast. From Bath to Lisbon Falls, where Grandfather would meet us with the horse for the ride out to the farm, we had a choice of steamcars or electric trolley. It was an easy trip, and all things considered better than coming out of Boston on a train.

It was the year I started school, and Dad took me into Raymond's store in Boston and bought me a complete cold-weather outfit for my trip to Maine. His father, my grandfather, knew we were coming, and away we sailed on the *Governor Cobb*.

The *Governor Cobb* was lovely. She was ablaze with lights at the pier. A steward showed us our cabin and Dad made me ready for bed—I had the upper berth and I wasn't, of course, about to sleep a wink all night. When the engines throbbed and we got under way the rhythm teased me into a fitful doze, but when we passed Cape Ann there was a roll that spoiled that. The stateroom became unbearably hot, and the reek of paint didn't help things much. I heard Dad say, "I can't seem to find any way to shut off the steam; maybe I can open the porthole." A light came on, and I looked from my berth to see Dad in a split-tail Cal Coolidge nightshirt fumbling at the port latch. He finally banged the wing nut with the heel of his shoe to start the paint, and gradually the stateroom cooled. But now I could hear the swish of water along the side of the vessel, and for a long time I stared at the place where the porthole had been. That's how I happened to see Seguin Light as we passed. "We'll be there soon," my father said. I think he didn't sleep much, either.

Not wanting to lose a tide, the stewards hustled everybody ashore at Bath, and the *Governor Cobb* was on her way downstream before we had walked over to the railroad station. I was warm enough in my new Raymond's outfit, but my cheeks went white in the morning Maine air, and I felt the chill in my lungs when I breathed. The sun was up, but a late-December sun does little active work in Maine and is dispirited and reluctant. Dad half-trotted me to the steamcars and we climbed into a coach that was just as hot as the stateroom had been. We would ride twenty miles to Lisbon Falls.

But we were to pause at Brunswick for breakfast. On the branch line, coming up from Bath, nobody knew Dad. But his main-line train ran through Brunswick, a junction, and there he was an old friend to everybody. A mail porter greeted him first, and the woman behind the depot lunch counter said, "Aren't you on the wrong train, Frank?"

I remember a roly-poly man with a green eyeshade behind the ticket window, who when Dad introduced me came out around through a door to shake my hand. He was the telegraph operator, and he said, "Welcome to Maine!"

"Aren't you working late, Sam?" my father said, and Sam said, "No, I go off at eight." So it was before eight o'clock that I tucked away my first breakfast in Maine—porridge, egg, bacon, fries, milk, and jelly doughnut. Then we were back in the hot-steam coach on our way up the Androscoggin Valley.

Dad was born on that old farm and grew up there. The house was a four-square "shingle palace" built by his grandfather. So Dad had communicated to me already a good part of his enthusiasm about "coming home." When the train stopped at Lisbon Falls, he looked through the unfrosted part of a windowpane and said, "He's here!" I was about to meet my grandfather. I looked out the window and I saw a horse and sleigh. The sleigh was really a pung, but I wasn't to know that distinction for a long time. A fur robe lay over the back of the seat. The horse had his head down, giving his attention to the hitching weight on the end of his strap. His muzzle was encrusted with rime frost. He looked frozen, and I was to learn later that his indifference was equally rigid. A blanket had been thrown over him.

Grandfather was in the station, soaking up heat from the potbelly to last the two and a half miles home, and he and Dad embraced. Grampie was a small man, and as he wore a full beard I have never thought of him as being young. He always looked old to me in his whiskers. He lifted me in his arms and gave me a bear hug that was almost painful even with my new mackinaw. He hugged me again and again. My middle name is Thomas, after him, and he kept saying, "Oh, Johnny-Tom. Oh, Johnny-Tom!"

The ride to the farm was a cruel experience. The platform thermometer at the railroad station said twenty-eight below zero, but Grampie said it had "warmed up" some. Tanty, short for Tantrabogus, was an aged horse and had long ceased to be interested in anything. When we had the blanket off, the weight taken in, and were on the pung seat, Tanty gave a great lurch to unstick the runners, but as they hadn't frozen down on that occasion he just about jerked us out of our boots. Then he settled into the monotony of lifting this foot and that foot, and Hamlet's ghost might well have told a hundred while Tanty decided which to set down first. Grandfather would yell "Hi, hi!" now and then, which Tanty disregarded. Dad, concerned about me, soon had me down off the seat and walking with him behind, to keep things circulating, and I told him I had pins and needles in my fingers. But I remember the way Tanty's bell clacked. In the wicked-fierce cold, there was no tone to the harness bell. When Tanty managed to move enough so the bell clacked, I would count, numb-fashion, and I counted clacks to the farm.

Grampie left us to go into the house and took Tanty to the barn. Through the back door and the summer kitchen, we came into the real kitchen, which was warm. A "black mogul" cookstove had been set into the colonial fireplace whole, so it was mostly out of the kitchen under the chimney, and Grampie had stoked it before he went to the depot. An iron teakettle was steaming. Dad shoved in new wood, hefted the kettle to see if it needed water, and began bringing me back to life. He chafed my hands and then had me hold them to my cheeks. He pulled off my boots but told me not to warm my feet too fast or I'd have chilblains. I'd never heard of chilblains before. I was well on the road to recovery when Grampie came in from the barn, his whiskers a solid sheet of ice. He had six hen's eggs in his pocket, but they had frozen and broken open.

The kitchen had a flavor that was new to me. In winter, in those days, farm kitchens all had it. It came from closing off the rest of the house and living beside the stove. The aroma was a combination of wood smoke and hot iron, lingering cookery, drying mittens and socks, warming boots, barn clothes, wintering geraniums on the window sills, and the relaxed effluence of a lazy beagle toasting under the stove. This kitchen, so very different from my mother's neat kitchen back in Massachusetts, was deficient in that very difference—there was no woman here; Grandfather had lived alone for years. In what Grandfather said was "the heat of the day," we left the kitchen and went to see his stock in the barn. I found Tanty in his stall, sound asleep. I was cautioned about the bull, but was encouraged to scratch the cows behind their horns, between their ears. They liked that. I got a good butt from a calf tied at the wall. Grampie had his ram with the sheep, but he cornered him and tied him up so I could walk among the ewes without his butting me. It was so cold the hens didn't risk frozen feet by scratching the litter, and were on the roosts. I found four more eggs, but they were broken, too. And Grampie let me toss some ears of yellow corn to the pigs, who were grateful. "The heat of the day" was a joke, and it was great to be back in the warm kitchen. That was a long day for me, and Dad got me ready for bed right after the chicken-stew supper. Grampie went out in the shed and found a soapstone that hadn't been warmed in years and set it on the stove. I took it to bed, wrapped in a towel.

When I was ready, soapstone in hand, Grampie tousled my head and Dad opened the door into the hall. We went up by kerosene lamp to a bedroom that had known no heat since the previous August. Dad said, "Now, the bed will warm up pretty soon, and you stay there until I come for you." I realized afterwards that he didn't mean to come for me until he had the kitchen warm with a new fire in the morning. The bed did grow warm with the soapstone and my body heat, but not right away. When it did, I slept, and I slept on after the exhaustion of that long day until daylight. I looked out from my comfortables just as Dad came for me.

Grampie had finished his barn chores and was by the stove, with red suspenders over his red underwear, stirring scrambled eggs. Dad had made hot biscuits, and Grampie had gone "down sulla" to fetch up a comb of honey. There was home-cured ham, and this had converted the beagle into a pointer—he had come from under the stove and was staring at the platter. I saw three ironstone mugs on the table, and when Grampie decanted the coffee he filled them all. I had never tasted coffee before—Mother said it wasn't good for children—but that morning I thought it was very good, indeed. That breakfast, I realize now, was the only thing about this visit to Maine that anybody in his right mind would account enjoyable. I had suffered with everything else.

Tanty didn't carry us back to town. Horace Jordan came by with a smart roader pulling a patent-leather cutter, and we rode in with him. The weather had moderated and it was only ten below—quite pleasant. The horse stepped along at a trot, and his bells jingled. We returned to Boston on the *Calvin Austin*, another white boat of the Eastern Steamship Line.

"Did you have a good time?" asked my mother.

I suppose mothers have an inward yearning that when their little boys first go away from home they will be, at least a little, homesick. When I was six I didn't suppose that. I do know, now, that I remember that visit to Maine, when I was six, because so many things happened that nobody would forget.

"Did you miss me?" she asked.

"Grampie has whiskers!" I said.

She hugged me, but it was a gentle hug and not a real squeezer like Grampie's. I had missed her, but not the way she thought. What I hadn't missed was the *Governor Cobb* and the bull and the dog under the stove and the soapstone and the pins and needles in my fingers and the honey and hot biscuits, and Tanty. And yes—the first war story Grampie ever told me, as he showed me the Gettysburg musket that stood in the kitchen corner.

Rio? No. I'd take the *Governor Cobb* again.

TWENTY

Not too long ago, W. W. Norton & Company, Inc., publisher of books in New York, was asking for a writer to do a book that would be "a demonstration of the fact that our military leaders are consistently wrong in their assessments [and] bad in execution and an investigation of why our system turns out military leaders of that caliber." During World War II, I was classified as a farmer, and mostly grew green beans for the Portland Packing Company and lend-lease, enduring noncombat indignities no soldier would believe, so I never came to get much acquainted with military leaders. I did get acquainted with things like the Office of Price Administration and the War Production Board. There were, for instance, the six thousand ration tickets the OPA gave me, each good for one gallon of gasoline for my tractor and I had to sign my name on each ticket. There was no gasoline available in our area anyway, and if a filling station happened to get some it was soon taken up by patriotic villagers who got there before the farmers. The villagers got tickets good for five gallons apiece, and they didn't have to sign them. But I did meet General Smith, and if I might have a second time around and see him again, perhaps I could do that book for W. W. Norton.

The chap here in Maine who was doing publicity for the Department of Sea and Shore Fisheries, Dick Reed, got drafted and became a soldier. This was not altogether an astute move by our government, inasmuch as our fisheries had taken on new importance with the conflict, and needed a good spokesman to state the case. But off he went, and our state house called me to ask if I would fill in and do Dick's work until they could find a replacement. I agreed to put in a day or two a week, at my own time, and found out immediately that while Dick had enjoyed something of a sinecure, the new importance of sea food made a lot more work. The armed services were calling for more and more fish. Civilians were urged to turn to fish to save on red meat. And then the idiocy of lend-lease went after canned sea food for the Russians. Just as all the vacant buildings from Kittery to Eastport opened up to handle the new demands, the WPB stepped in and restricted everything. Nobody ever needed a spokesman to tell the story more that the fishermen of Maine did in those days. The sea and shore commissioner at that time was Arthur Greenleaf of Boothbay Harbor, who sat on his duff and was no particular use to anybody. Well, he had a good job and he was indifferent. When an occasion came along when he might have made an appearance, he'd send somebody to represent him, and that's how I came to meet General Smith.

I'm pretty sure his name was Smith. He was in command of the United States Army installations in the Portland area. Since the Civil War, the army interest in that vicinity had been an antiquated fort that retained the honor of supplying a color guard for the parade every Memorial Day. But Portland harbor was now an assembly point for supply vessels to be convoyed to Europe, so the army took a new lease on life and faced up. General Smith was not Maine—I would suggest Middle West—and when he arrived to assume command it was something like the changing of the guard at Buckingham Palace. He really took command. And now he found that he was faced with stiff competition. The maritime activity had first importance, and he was definitely outranked by the United States Navy and the United States Marine Corps. I didn't know anything about this status problem until later, because I was down east doing my best to save the fisheries. I had to have a coast guard ID card before I could look at the ocean, and every precaution was taken to save America. Early on, I decided it doesn't take much to be a spy. Tightest secrecy prevailed about the sailing of the convoys from Portland harbor. But we knew that whenever a truckload of tinned alewives left Stonington, the convoy would sail in two days.

As soon as this General Smith got some oil on his swivel chair, he announced that he was going to commandeer Custom House Wharf and make it into an army depot. The navy, you see, had taken a wharf on the Portland water front, and so had the coast guard and so had the marines, and General Smith of the United States Army wanted a wharf, too. He had no need of a wharf, but that wasn't the point. Custom House Wharf was the only wharf left that could serve the nonmilitary uses of Portland, and just about everything that was left of harbor traffic was using it. The Portland Fish Company was out on the end, and it was from Portland Fish that we heard of the general's announcement. The company was not only doing its usual peacetime work but had taken on military supply, and one of its customers was General Smith. "What can be done?" was the way we heard it.

Now, as far as any valid importance in the war effort at that time may be taken under scrutiny at this time, General Smith might just as well have been custodian of an outhouse in a Maine lumber camp. But he conducted himself as a true prophet of the Lord, and to objectors he simply repeated that the decision had been made and Custom House Wharf would be an army depot. He, General Smith, had spoken. A few concerned people suggested that perhaps he had made a small boo-boo and should reconsider, but General Smith stood like Julius Caesar at the other side of the Rubicon. It was clear, soon enough, that not only would the Maine fisheries be in trouble because of General Smith but many other important interests would suffer. For one, the Casco Bay Lines. This was a fleet of freight and passenger boats that worked between Custom House Wharf and the islands. South Portland had a big shipyard, making Liberty Ships for the war effort, and something like fifteen thousand people were involved, most of them living out on the islands. In a few days the howl about General Smith was substantial, and he agreed to meet representative spokesmen and explain his situation— meantime hearing their remarks. I was sent to represent the Sea and Shore Department.

About as good a place as we have in Maine for a genteel and excellent meal is the Cumberland Club in Portland. It's not a public place, but being a guest there is easy enough, and this seemed a good place to confer with General Smith. I arrived just short of noon to find a considerable and agitated assembly that was ready and eager to confront the general. City, county, and state officials were there, along with the owners of little businesses and the lawyers of big businesses on the wharf. There came a bustle at the door, and into the luncheon room came General Smith.

He was a large man, tailored well in the grandeur of his rank, and medaled like a Christmas tree. But he did suggest a French barber, and his severe military bearing had a ladylike lah-de-dah. He wore his hanky up his sleeve. The luncheon was the usual Cumberland Club delight. When the general at last touched his fingers together before him and was ready to listen, the fish dealers spoke. I followed, offering statistics supplied by the department I was representing, but the general wasn't listening and I soon sat down. A lawyer for the Casco Bay Lines spoke, then somebody for the shipyard, and I remember there was a spokesman for Boone's Restaurant. The total simply showed that if General Smith insisted, a whole great lot of people were going to be in trouble.

General Smith now awoke, drew forth his hanky and touched it artistically to his lips, said that his mind had been made up and he was not about to change it, and that he certainly did want to thank one and all for such a lovely luncheon. He arose and marched forth, keeping step with himself all the way.

Before he got to the door, the lawyer for the Casco Bay Lines said, "O.K., General—and as soon as I return to my office the Casco Bay Lines fleet will go on mooring and stay there until you do change it."

The general paused at the door, but he didn't turn to look back.

"And," said the lawyer, "I think it will be well for you to figure out between now and five o'clock about getting fifteen thousand people back and forth to the islands."

The general moved along.

It worked. General Smith did not take over Custom House Wharf. I hadn't thought of him in a long time, but he came to mind when I read that appeal by W. W. Norton & Company, Inc., publisher. On another time around I could study him more closely and write that book.

TWENTY-ONE

Eddie Skillin and I were of an age and shared many a Tom Sawyer adventure. Some of them I'd like to try again, but most of all it would be wonderful if, on another time around, we might find the Freeport cannon. Eddie and I always believed we did find it, but circumstances well beyond our control prevented our proving that we had. Eddie lived in the village and I was a little ways out, so we arranged our private signal for when excitement was afoot and one wanted the other. We had a whistle. Our whistle came from the beautiful call of the wood thrush. Years afterwards we learned that our whistle amounted to the first four notes of "O Canada," but in our time Canadians sang "The Maple Leaf Forever" and Eddie and I didn't know about "O Canada." When I heard a wood thrush I would go out to find Eddie waiting for me, and he would appear if I whistled at his house.

For a number of years Eddie and I would go on a walking trip each summer just before school opened. There wasn't much chance to hitchhike then, so we walked. We had a World War pup tent—it came in two pieces and buttoned at the peak. Eddie had one side in his pack and I the other, and wherever we were in late afternoon we'd button the tent together, string it on lobster-trap "pot-warp" between two trees, make a fir bed, lay out our paper-mill felt blankets, and fight mosquitoes all night. We always found something to amuse us, and after a week or so we'd hike home and get ready for school. One year we were hiking up the Sebasticook River and we came to a place that fairly cried out for us to stop. It was the most likely place for a camp that anybody could ask for. A little swift water, then a pool with a wide sandy beach. As we came upon this scene, a trout leaped in the pool. We spent the night.

While we were making our breakfast the next morning, and

waiting for our small fire to die down to embers, Eddie poked in the sand and found an arrow point. We became archeologists on the spot, and during the next hour of so dug up eight pounds of relics from the Stone Age. The eight pounds were established by the postmaster at Harmony, because we found a box and mailed our treasure home. Not all the points were good, but some were, and two–three got into museums. Eddie's father was a gem buff and made some pieces into pendants on golden chains—I believe my sister still has one. And, now we knew why that spot on the Sebasticook seemed so ideal for a camp. For thousands of years people had passed up and down that river, and here was the favorite stopping place—the best spot on the route. This was the place. And Eddie and I probably left our record there as had so many others.

There was another special occasion worth repeating. Eddie whistled under my window long after I'd been asleep. I sat up, got up, dressed, and went down to find Eddie on our back porch. It was a sharp winter night, with a good snow cover. "Northern lights!" Eddie said, and I looked up to see the sky awave with long, wavering streamers. We trudged through the snow to the rear of our buildings, to get away from the reflection of a street lamp down the way, and put up a short ladder to get onto the roof of our henhouse. There wasn't much pitch to the north side of the henhouse, so we laid ourselves back in the snow and had a full view of the sky. This may well have been the finest display of my time. Off the north came the great waves of colored light to pass over our heads and out into the south. The forty-fifth parallel of north latitude crosses Maine, so this meant the streamers were moving better than halfway to the equator. Mostly, in Maine, a display of these lights will fade soon, but this one went on and on, and Eddie and I had been on our backs a great while before things tapered off and the stars grew brighter. I remember we didn't come down off the roof right away, but stayed there in some sort of respect—we didn't want to break the spell. Then Eddie went home and I went back to bed—to find that my bed had cooled and I had to warm it a second time in one night. As my teeth chattered, I replayed the show in the sky—it was a night to remember.

I was eating breakfast the next morning when my father came in from feeding the hens. He wanted to know if I had any idea what two idiots had been doing in the snow up on the henhouse roof. The evidence was there, and it puzzled him. My easy explanation brought him considerable relief.

The Freeport cannon was a major campaign. Right after the Civil War a great number of surplus cannon were made available to communities throughout the North for memorial purposes. A town would buy a statue, flank it with two cannon, and dedicate a park to the memory of the Boys in Blue. Freeport did this. The statue was Number 48 from a stonecutter's catalog—a simple infantryman standing at ease with his musket. The statue is still there; the soldier is looking down South Street, on perpetual post. The wooden wheels of the two cannon weathered away many years ago, and cement bases were put under them. The cannon balls remain. So long as the Grand Army of the Republic functioned, the annual Freeport Decoration Day speeches were made beside this statue.

At the time of delivery, a long trainload of cannon came up to Maine. The train would pause at the depot while two cannon were unlashed from a flatcar and rolled to the platform. Then the train would go on to the next town to leave two more. At Freeport, the train crew got the town's two cannon off, and nobody knew that a bunch of boys had sneaked off a third from away back on the end of the train. They tipped it into the bushes near the old coal pockets and allowed the train to proceed. Thus Freeport came to have two cannon for the park and a third for the boys to play with. And that's just it. From the day it arrived until the first decade of the twentieth century, the third cannon was a Freeport tradition. Since it had been acquired in stealth, it remained so. After the train pulled out, the boys who had hijacked it took it apart. The barrel was cast iron and it took many hands to lift it. The two wheels were hidden in two haymows, the tailpiece in another, and the barrel was greased, wrapped in burlap, and buried up on Torrey's Hill. It remained hidden thus until the night before the next Fourth of July, when it was brought out, assembled, and used to salute the occasion. When it went off it just about blew Freeport apart, and as the article was contraband it had to be moved before anybody in authority could arrive. Trundled to another part of town, it spoke again, and was moved again. After American Independence had been suitably saluted, the boys took the gun apart and hid it again. Thus things went for quite a few years, until the "boys" were no longer exactly that.

So the story goes, and Eddie and I heard it in our time, as all Freeport boys had heard it in theirs. One year while the village boys were making the cannon ready for the Fourth, some interlopers from South Freeport came in an organized assault and stole the cannon. And from then on, for a few years, the cannon changed hands now and then. On the last Fourth that it spoke, it was in the hands of the boys from South Freeport, and afterwards they took it apart and hid it as usual—tradition says the barrel, well greased, was buried in the chip pile at the shipyard. But on the next Fourth, the gun was not brought out. Instead, the boys from South Freeport played a trick. They took a stick of dynamite, added a fuse, and wrapped it tightly in wet oakum—making a bomb. When they touched the bomb off, the boys from the village thought the cannon had spoken, and they raced around all night looking for it. Every half hour or so the boys from the harbor would touch off another bomb, and so it went.

For some reason I can't remember now, Eddie and I were talking one day with Mr. Joseph E. Davis. He had been a young man on the occasion of the cannon's last appearance, and he had seen it buried in the chip pile at the shipyard. Much elderly to Eddie and me, he told what he knew of the story, and he added that while the cannon never came out to be fired again, it had not remained in the chip pile. Some years later, after bombs had taken its place, the cannon was taken up, re-greased, and buried under the dirt floor of a cellar. Mr. Davis was not present, and knew this by hearsay. It was one or the other of several South Freeport cellars, somewhere near the Stone Post, but he didn't know for sure. It wasn't a matter of his memory—Mr. Davis was still keen of mind. He just never really knew except what he'd heard.

Eddie and I made a project of finding the cannon. We spent a lot of time and did a lot of hunting. We narrowed the houses down, and decided on three. We found there was a certain reluctance on the part of householders to let two boys go down in their cellars and shove rods in the dirt. For one thing, South Freeport property was coming into its own as suburban to Portland, and a new kind of resident was shaping up. By that time, not too many people knew about the old cannon. Sounded to them like a fairy tale. But we did decide that if Mr. Davis (now no longer with us) had been right, it had to be a certain home. We applied.

The gentleman who owned the house had "restored" it when he bought, a few years back. This restoration had included a new hot-water heating system with a consequent rearrangement of the basement. Eddie and I winced when we heard a cellar called a basement. The dirt floor under which the cannon, undoubtedly, had been buried was now four inches of cement. Besides, the furnace sat exactly where Eddie and I had projected our find.

Eddie isn't here now, either, and since those days the metal-detector has been perfected. I wonder. . . .

TWENTY-TWO

Quite a few down-Maine "lanches" have been my luck—
my first was in 1919, when the five-masted *Sintram* went
into the tide at South Freeport. I was on her deck and it wasn't
really much fun—it was a cold February day and those of us
aboard in the official launch party nigh froze to death before a
boat came to take us off. I did, I suppose, learn to pronounce
launch that day. Mainers lanch boats, and if you look at Long-
fellow's "The Building of the Ship" you will find that he, good
Mainer, rhymed *launch* with *stanch*. A lanch is a tremendous
thrill, even with the smaller vessels Maine now, occasionally,
makes. In the days of real sail a lanch was an occasion for a town
holiday, and I'm happy to say that in our town of Friendship
the school children are "let out" whenever Lash's boat yard puts
a new craft in the water. It's heartening to see the youngsters
coming with picnic baskets, led by their teachers, and after the
boat is afloat they have a picnic on the shore.

Maine's maritime historian, William Hutchinson Rowe, tells
of a launch in the old days:

> The launch of such a vessel was a great event. In Sep-
> tember, 1878, the Cushing and Briggs yard in Freeport put
> afloat the *John A. Briggs.* This launching of Freeport's larg-
> est ship was a red-letter day. As great a number of people
> gathered to see her floated as ever witnessed a launch in
> Casco Bay. From the surrounding countryside they came
> in all manner of conveyances, from carriages to oxcarts.
> The Maine Central Railroad ran a special train, and two or
> three island steamers brought crowds from Portland and
> the Foresides, while the river was white with sailboats from
> Harpswell, Brunswick, and the Islands. The papers esti-
> mated that over seven thousand people were present. The

governor of the state, Alonzo Garcelon, was there—also James A. Garfield, who was scheduled for a campaign speech in Yarmouth later in the day. Never having seen a launch, he drove over to see the *Briggs* take the water.

The launch of the *Sintram* tried to recapture much of that. But the *Sintram* was the very last large vessel to be built in Maine and there would be no more old-time lanches except for the Liberty Ships during World War II and the continuing production of steel vessels at Bath. I would not care to repeat the *Sintram* experience—I didn't warm up until along in July. The lanch I would like to reproduce on another time around was not a lanch at all—it was called a christening, and that, of course, is incorrect. Children are christened; boats are named.

William Hilton was a pioneer forester, our first fire warden. He came to manage timberlands for the Great Northern Paper Company and was a legend in the Maine woods in his own time. Beside the road to Rockwood, just outside of Greenville Junction, there is a monument to his memory—he manned the country's first fire warden's tower, on Squaw Mountain. And when the Great Northern Paper Company had a new towboat built for bringing boomed pulpwood across Chesuncook Lake, the boat was named for William Hilton. She was quite a boat. Mostly, she was engines—twin diesels that probably could have towed the Empire State Building over to New Jersey. There's an old story Flats Jackson tells about the time he was cooking on a towboat—not the *William Hilton*—and they towed into the wind for seven hours and wound up five miles behind the starting place. Thousands and thousands of cords of pulpwood would be impounded in the great booms, and it took power to start them along. The *William Hilton* had that power. She was built at salt water in East Boothbay, carried by truck to Chesuncook Dam in two pieces, and welded together there. She was already in the water when Great Northern staged a big party at the Dam. Bill Pelletier, the cook, even made a bean hole. The weather was ideal. The crowd assembled.

My wife and I packed our woodland gear and attended. We pitched our tent at the excellent campground then manicured by Forestry Warden Oscar Gagnon, and Oscar made us welcome in his affable way. We would stay a few days, including the one of the so-called christening. That's an interesting region. When Ripogenus Dam was built in 1927, it flowed back one of the largest man-made lakes in the world. Ripogenus Lake and Caribou Lake became one with Chesuncook Lake, and an older dam at Chesuncook outlet was covered with water. It is still there, although invisible, and the area retains the name of Chesuncook Dam. The depot camp that went with the days of river driving is still there, and Chesuncook Dam is the location of the memorial to the river driver. He is long gone, timber now moves on highways by truck, the towboat *William Hilton* is now a party boat at Boothbay Harbor. Bought by Captain Elliot Winslow of that resort harbor, it carries summer folks around the bay at so much a ticket.

For anybody with any kind of salt-water background, the exercises putting the *William Hilton* in commission were interesting—even amusing. There was complete lack of the usual nautical lingo. The woodsmen who were to operate her knew their own trade, but not that of 'longshore folks. The galley on the *William Hilton* was called the cookshack. William Hilton's granddaughter was given a bottle of champagne to swing, and it had been sitting in the sun on the pier all forenoon. "What am I supposed to do?" she asked, and from the back of the crowd came the soft-spoken instructions of a veteran woodsman, "Poleax her!" She did, the bottle of champagne burst, and so well did it fizz that never a drop came down. The champagne just disappeared in the air. Then everybody turned and went up to the boomhouse for Bill's banquet.

It was a real display, and the bean-hole beans were superb. Then the crowd thinned out—most everybody else had a distance to go—and we retired across the way to our tent in Oscar's compound. We were joined there in a few minutes by Mr. and Mrs. Hastings N. Bartley, Jr., of Millinocket, whom we had just met at the dinner table. We had suggested they join us for the jolly hour. So we had a folding table arranged, with chairs, and the essentials of said hour, and there we sat right by the road where we could wave good-by to those who passed on their way home.

You've heard of Percival P. Baxter. He donated the land for Baxter State Park. He had been governor of Maine for two terms in the 1920s, and now was our senior resident philanthropist. Majestic Mount Katahdin, in his park, stands as his principal monument, and on the day the *William Hilton* ceremonies brought us to Chesuncook Dam we could look from our tent site and Katahdin. In his later years, Mr. Baxter used to make an annual visitation to his park. He'd come from Portland in a limousine, with chauffeur, and he'd take two–three of his cronies for a ride, and they'd spend a few days looking at the mountain. Back when Mr. Baxter was acquiring the land he was to give to Maine as a park, he negotiated for a lot of it with William Hilton. So, being in the area, he was invited to the exercises for the new boat. Being invited, he came. And Bun and Jayne Bartley and my wife and I sat there and watched the big black automobile start up and come along towards us on its way. "I move we stand up for Uncle Percy," I said, and we stood up.

As the limousine came abreast of us, it stopped. Uncle Percy nodded at us through the window, but kept his seat. On the far side the door opened, a man got out, and he came around the back of the automobile to duck under Oscar's split-cedar fence. He walked directly up to our little table, reached his hand out to Bun Bartley, and he said, "I heard you were here Mr. Gould, and I want to shake your hand. I've been reading your books, and I want you to know I enjoy them."

Bun wrung his hand in evident pleasure. "Glad to hear things like that," Bun said. "Thank you very much."

"Yes, sir," said the man, "this is indeed a pleasure. When they told me you were here, I asked the Governor to pause a moment so I could speak to you. Given me a lot of pleasure; keep up the good work!"

"Thank you again," said Bun. "I'd like you to meet Mrs. Gould," and he indicated Jayne, his own wife.

"A pleasure," said the man.

"And these are Mr. and Mrs. Bartley from Millinocket," said Bun Bartley, and he gestured our way. My wife said, "So nice," and I said, "How do you do?"

"Well, mus'n't keep the Governor waiting," said the man as he started to take his leave. "I'm so pleased to have this minute with you."

"And I'm so pleased you wanted to pause," said Bun.

The limousine purred out of sight.

"Who the hell was *that?*" I asked.

"One of *my* devoted readers," said Bun.

Then he said, "I'm not sure, but I think that was Judge Murray. Oscar was close by and Bun called to him, "Who was that?"

Oscar called back, "That was Judge Murray."

Edward P. Murray of Bangor was an associate justice of the Maine Supreme Judicial Court, retiring on April 6, 1948. He went to his grave believing he had shaken my hand at Chesuncook Dam the day the *William Hilton* was "lanched."

Do you wonder that the Bartleys and the Goulds remain close friends?

TWENTY-THREE

Over the years, now and then, I've connected with a deer and we have a venison winter. Mostly, though, I'm not much of a hunter and I don't see much game. I have no particular compunction about taking a deer, and mistrust the humane tendencies of people who lament shooting the poor little thing. It's not easy to explain things to somebody who wouldn't know the differences anyway. The deer can be merely an excuse to roam the woods, watch the woodpeckers, eat hearty meals, and lie in a bedroll listening to treesqueaks. In the same way a trout makes it reasonable to walk up a brook. I drew some of my earlier conclusions about this one evening when the lady on my right gave me a tender plea for the beautiful deer and she was eating roast beef. Well, be that as it may, a hunting trip can be a miserably unpleasant experience, and I well remember one of mine that the lovers of deer may wish I should endure again, just to teach me a good lesson.

The time my father and I took the groceries up to Lydia Gifford was not, I think, a hunting trip. We had eleemosynary intentions and our interest was diverted to the amusement of the Queen's Arm. A few years before that Dad and I went on a real hunting trip, and unless it would please the preservationists I would just as lief not repeat it. I was in college and he was still a young man.

He finished his week's railway mail run in Bangor just before the Armistice Day weekend. I was there with the Model T when he got off the train and we headed for Masardis up in Aroostook County. Dad had heard of somebody up that way who "took in" hunters, and had made arrangements. It was a long ride. We found the place, a farmhouse on the only road, and a woman welcomed us and showed us a room. This farmhouse was a kind of base camp, used by hunters when they arrived and departed.

The hunting camp itself was at the end of a six-mile walk over an abandoned lumber-camp tote road and was in fact a building once used by a chopping crew. There was also a loghaul, equally abandoned, that wound around through the swamps and used up fourteen miles to cover the same distance as the tote road. The woman gave us supper—boiled venison in gravy slathered on boiled potatoes, hot biscuits, strong tea, and cold apple pie. Winter hadn't really set in yet and the days were mild, but our bedroom window was nailed shut and a blanket hung over it. We slept all right. At daylight we got up and had breakfast—boiled venison in gravy slathered on boiled potatoes, hot biscuits, strong tea, and cold apple pie.

The six-mile walk to camp could be done in about two hours, but we hunted along the way and used up the forenoon. Never saw a thing—not even a "sign." We got to the camp just at noon and had a fine dinner of boiled venison in gravy slathered on boiled potatoes, hot biscuits, strong tea, and cold apple pie. That afternoon we hunted up and down the stream by the camp, didn't see anything, and came in for a supper of boiled venison in gravy slathered on boiled potatoes, hot biscuits, strong tea, and cold apple pie. We played cribbage by a kerosene lamp until bedtime, slept, and had breakfast of the familiars. Dad and I agreed that we had made a mistake and returning to civilization would be a sound plan. Since we had seen no game coming in on the tote road, we elected to depart by the loghaul, and with sandwiches made of biscuits and boiled venison in our pockets we set out.

Remnants of loghauls may still be seen in certain parts of the Maine wilderness. They were graded roadways built for the sled-trains of long logs that were pulled by the steam tractors called Lombards. The lore of the Lombards, belonging to the early years of the twentieth century, needs no recitation here, but the nature of a loghaul is important. Being graded, it held to level ground and usually took advantage of swamps and bogs. Logs were laid in crosswise of the roadway, close together, so the succession of ridges suggested corduroy cloth, and such construction was, and is, called corduroy. Dirt and snow smoothed the surface, so the sledloads of logs moved serenely along much as a freight train rides the rails. In use in winter, a loghaul would be iced by a crew sprinkling water. But this loghaul hadn't been used in years; the dirt was gone between logs. The logs were rotting. We found ourselves stepping along from log to log, negotiating corduroy like a tramp walking railroad ties. If we missed a log, our feet went through the light crust of early ice, and we'd go to our knees in swamp water. After a mile or so our feet were folding and unfolding with each log like a hen grasping the roost. And by the time we knew the loghaul was not good for us, we were far enough along so returning were as tedious as go o'er. We kept on. We saw no game. Had we seen any, we'd have been fools to shoot because of getting the meat out over that torture. We ate our biscuits and venison, rested, and moved along.

It began to come on to dark and we had no idea how much farther to the Masardis road. Every muscle was strained and groaning. Our feet hurt straight back to the napes of our necks. Our shinbones throbbed like banjo strings. Log by log we kept on, desperately hoping we might make the highway before complete darkness made us grope for our footing. And we came out just about as night shut down. Dad said, "I never was so sore in my life, but I'm hungry enough to relish that damned stewed venison."

I found it sort of shaky to walk again on pure ground, and I was testing my steps. I said, "Wouldn't you rather have a platter of pork steak with some French fries?"

My father didn't say anything right away, and then he said I was lucky he didn't shoot me.

We could now see the lights of the farmhouse down the road, and we arrived to enjoy a hearty supper of boiled venison in gravy slathered on boiled potatoes, hot biscuits, strong tea, and cold apple pie. The next morning we passed up breakfast and headed downstate.

And we stopped in Bangor to go into the Bangor Exchange Hotel for a couple of sirloin steaks.

TWENTY-FOUR

When my son married Bill's daughter, going on two
decades ago, Bill and I commenced a happy custom of
disappearing together into the Maine woods every July. After
grandson William was born (there is now also Thomas; we share
two), we began calling this the Annual Grandfathers' Retreat.
The first year we pitched a wall tent at Baker Lake, where the
long St. John River may be said to commence. This is far up in
International Paper Company timberlands, a few miles from Ste.
Aurélie on the Quebec boundary. We took my precious canvas
guide's canoe (an early White), made our meals over open fires,
and had ourselves one whale of a time. But afterwards we were
privileged to use a timberland company camp down at Caucomagomac Lake dam—a tight building left over from a lumber-camp
complex long abandoned. Now and then the timberland company needs a place to shelter cruisers, scalers, dam tenders, and
other workmen on special jobs, so this camp is kept equipped.
It has propane-gas refrigeration, lamps, and range. The beds
have foam mattresses, and the cupboards are full of table and
cooking dishes. The front yard is Cauc Lake. We have it made.
In late years we have left the canoe home and take with us a
fourteen-foot skiff I made; it has a two-horse outboard. We don't
miss the paddle work a bit. The skiff fits into my pickup truck
with ample room for the gear, wangan, and comforts to which
we are accustomed. It may be that the young folks worry about
these two old codgers going off alone to rough it amid the dan-
gers of the uncharted wilderness, and we make a point of not
telling them how the cook at the Scott Brook lumber camp, ten
miles away, sends us over a loaf of new bread every morning.
Such hardships are endurable for the sake of our own good
company.

We make day trips and have explored that whole region

between the law and Canada, but we find we get all the angling we need right in Caucomagomac Stream below the dam—there is a fish ladder there and we have to do our casting 150 feet below the dam. A fish ladder is a succession of pools so arranged that a fish can pass up from one to another until he has surmounted the height of a dam. Otherwise, there would be no spawning runs above the dam. We obey this rule of 150 feet meticulously, because the game warden has become a fine friend of ours and we would dislike to put him to the pleasure of arresting us. Usually, a fish arriving from downstream will come to the fish ladder and wait a day or two before making the effort to climb. So a pool just below a fish ladder doesn't make sportsmanlike angling; hence the 150 feet. In addition to Cauc Stream, we have located a beaver flowage close by, and if the quick water fails us we can always wade in and pick up enough pan-trout for a breakfast, lunch, and chowder. This does not occupy us fully, however, and we give our attention to the cultural uplift of the North Woods. Our Caucomagomac Lake Institute of Fine & Coarse Art schedules lectures, seminars, conferences, classes, and numerous exhibitions to edify and adorn. Bastille Day usually comes during our visitation, and we conduct special exercises which include French toast for breakfast. I wouldn't want you to think Bill and I pass our time entirely in idle pleasure.

Since we do this every July, there is little point in speculating on the next time around. Bill and I agree that every visitation is better than the last, and we expect this to continue. Considering all our good times, there is really only one that can never be repeated, and that is the one I'd wish for on another time around. It was the day Bill caught his first salmon. It hadn't occurred to me that Bill had never taken a salmon. He had fished in Maine before I knew him, and the day I met him he was fishing at Kennebago Lake. Kennebago Lake is mighty fine salmon water, and I just assumed that Bill had caught one. But here we were fishing on Cauc Stream, and I had taken two very fine salmon just above the rips called The Horserace. Bill was admiring them, and he said, "I've never caught a salmon." It would be only a

matter of time, of course, so we whipped flies around and I
expected Bill would tie into his salmon any minute. He didn't.

Now, Big Scott Brook comes into the South Arm of Cauc Lake,

and a few miles above, Loon Stream flows into Big Scott Brook. Loon Stream drains Loon Lake. Maine has a number of Loon Lakes, but this is the one the Indians called Kwanoksangamack, which I think is pronounced "Chumley," and we're getting back up into the woods. At that time Loon Lake had a water-holding dam made of earth, with a spillway made of logs. The spillway had two gates. The old dam was going to pieces, and in 1978 the Great Northern Paper Company had to replace it with a concrete dam that included a fish ladder. But when I took Bill to fish at Loon Lake dam there was no fish ladder, and he could assault the pool where salmon would be somewhat at his mercy. As we walked toward the dam, I saw a salmon break water, and I put Bill in position so he would reach that spot.

Things went about as they should. I told Bill to let his fly drift in the quick water thus and so, and I climbed up over the dam to cross to the other side of the pool. I was directly opposite him, but we weren't fishing the same place. But after a few casts I laid my rod down and composed myself to see the show—I was certain Bill was about to tie into his heart's desire. He was making fine casts, and his Gray Ghost was making the right loop in the water to pass properly over what I considered the right place. It didn't happen right away, but there it was! The salmon rose, taking the fly on the way up, and he had it for sure. Bill deftly set the hook in mid-air, and the fish came down. The landlocked Maine salmon is by no means just another fish. He is spectacular in his action, and not an easy bombshell to bring to net. He comes clean out of water to shake himself, and his runs are speedy and brisk. He thinks nothing of snapping a leader or straightening out a hook. He's a crasher. And Bill was tied into a great-granddaddy crasher.

Bill certainly did everything right with his first one. He kept the rod tip up, the tension just right. When the salmon streaked away and the line zizz-zz-zz-ed in the water, he let go carefully, snubbing the charge up at the right moment. Bill took in line as needed turn by turn of his hand—never touched the reel. The game was far enough along now so that I could see Bill was going to bring in his first salmon, and I relaxed as I watched the show.

Thousands and thousands of sorry anglers have lost their first good fish by being overeager. Never "horse" a trout or salmon— don't derrick him. Give him his play, and let him go it. Take your time. Bill did everything just the way I would have done it—which is to say, the right way. I had no reason to call instructions, which he wouldn't have heard anyway because of the noise of the quick water. The salmon made five distinct runs, leaping each time and then taking out line. Bill had the finesse of a Jascha Heifetz on a concerto solo. I broke off a stem of grass to chew.

Beautiful!

Now Bill would have his salmon.

And now comes the duck. Up in those Maine lakes and ponds we don't see many of the waterfowl commoner along the coast. The principal duck is the American merganser, which Mainers have always called the sheldrake. Less often we see a relative, the hooded merganser. The hood, a tuft of feathers behind the head, is distinguishing. So, as I was at ease, well satisfied with Bill's performance, a lady hooded merganser decided to bring her summer's brood down from Loon Lake over the dirt dam to Loon Stream, and then down the waterway until in late season all would fly south from some place on the Penobscot River. In the manner of her kind this lady came through the bushes and appeared, flanked by her babies, right between Bill's feet as he stood playing his salmon. I could see all this, but she didn't know Bill was there and Bill didn't know she was there.

She now discovered Bill.

"Whark-k-k-k-k!"

This to her brood, and off they went down Loon Stream at 85 mph, bursting forth in great profusion.

I couldn't see that Bill noticed her. His rod tip stayed up, his tension was perfect, his salmon had turned and was about to come in. Bill didn't need a net with this one. He just worked the fish into shallow water and sort of led him ashore. Bill had his first salmon up on the grass and was laying down his rod.

I went back over the dam and came down to him. There he stood, mesmerized by the sight of a beautiful twenty-two-inch salmon. He looked up at me, his eyes misty—even glazed. He was performing correctly in the manner of one who has just taken his first salmon. He seemed to have lost some faculties. He opened his mouth to speak to me.

And in the manner of one just successful as aforesaid, he spoke thus: "Glah-glah-glah-glah-glah-glah."

"Nobody ever said it better," I said, and I pumped his hand. In a moment he was himself again, and he said, "Did you see that foolish duck?"

Surprised that Bill would have noticed the duck during his excitement, I said, "Eyah. Hooded merganser."

Bill said, "And fifteen little ones!"

He was right. She had fifteen little ones.

TWENTY-FIVE

There's a good deal of salt in ocean water—more than you'd think. I went to some pains to establish that, and the day I found it out I had much fun with Vic Coffin—this kind of fun is something any upright citizen will look forward to repeating. Salt from sea water was an important item of commerce in the early days of Maine, and my ancestor was a salt seller. He sold salt. He made salt. He had come to what was then Georgetown, on the New Meadows River, as part of the English establishment of shore-based fisheries. But he had a trade—he was a housewright—and he prospered as new settlers came along and wanted homes. He must have been alert to his opportunities, because before long he set up a "salt works" on the Brunswick side of the river, precisely where the playground of Thomas Point Beach is today. A salt works consisted of stone arches that supported cauldrons. At high tide the salt makers filled the cauldrons with sea water and kindled fires to cause evaporation. The fires under the arches were kept going until the cauldrons were dry, and the cauldrons would be filled again at the next high water. In the *History of Brunswick* by George Augustus Wheeler and Henry Warren Wheeler, there is a passage about the early salt works on the New Meadows River, even to giving prices paid per bushel for salt.

We have no certain knowledge of when Europeans first exploited the fisheries of the Gulf of Maine. Probably Scandinavian and Irish fishermen had been here well before Columbus, and for many years offshore islands had been bases for curing, packing, and shipping cod. When such activity came to the mainland—the "maine"—New Meadows River had early settlements. Salt for curing the fish was at first brought from Spain—a boat would leave, say, England, go to Spain for salt, cross to Maine, load fish, and return to England. This meant time, and as frictions came and went in the politics of Europe it was not always smart for an English vessel to approach Spain. My ancestor thus thought out his salt business and had a ready market in the vicinity. There's one record that some five hundred ships came from Europe in one season to load fish—at least some of it cured with my ancestor's salt.

When my grandfather told me how his great-grandfather made salt, I fell to wondering how much salt a man might make with three–four cauldrons boiling off between tides. Wood was cheap for the fires, but it had to be cut down, cut to stove size, and dried, so there was labor and time. Maple syrup, Grandfather said, will run about thirty to one, sap and syrup. But syrup is by no means down to sugar, and how much maple sugar would be had from thirty gallons of sap? Would thirty gallons of sea water give as much salt? I was doing my homework, you see. Then I found Wheeler's *History*, where salt was priced in shillings and pence. With the help of a teacher I came up with maybe a dollar a bushel, and in terms of the colonial economy this probably meant my ancestor was reasonably affluent. The question would come on how many bushels he could make on a tide. I was fifteen when I set up the big experiment on Flying Point beach at Freeport and boiled down ocean water to find out.

I carried Mother's big preserving kettle to the shore. I carried rocks to make an arch, just above the high-water mark. At high tide I filled the kettle, and I kindled my fire. Wood wasn't too much of a problem, as the Flying Point shore was littered with driftwood, and a good part of it was reasonably dry in the sun. Between stokings I gathered wood, and I soon had a pile big enough to last out the experiment. In almost no time I had a rolling boil going, and steam and smoke rose in a cloud.

In just about an hour Victor Coffin appeared. Vic lived there at Flying Point and everybody knew Vic. He clammed, and would buy clams for resale if we boys cared to earn a penny or two. Flying Point was not then the select seaside residential nicety of now, and I was not necessarily invading any privacies along shore. But Vic kept an eye on things, and I think he did have an appointment as town constable—more or less to make sure clam diggers were residents. I had dug clams for Vic, so he knew me and there was no formality of greeting.

"Saw smoke and surmised a fire," said Vic.

This seemed to me a reasonable process of thought, all things considered, and a conclusion so patently self-evident that it needed no embellishment from me. I stood up and put more wood on my fire. Vic tried to peer through the steam into Mother's preserving kettle, but could see only the bubbling top of the water. He blinked and said, "They's an old sayin'—where they's smoke, they's fi-yer."

"Generally is," I said, and I now realized I had Vic's curiosity to play around with. Then, again—after all—it wouldn't be easy to explain to Vic about colonial fisheries, an ancestor's occupation, a boy's wonderment. . . . I didn't say anything, and neither did Vic. Off towards Bustins Island a loon let go in the wild mocking laughter of a weird sister with a hex on the world. Lingering, prolonged, the eerie cry always makes the listener pause. I was looking off towards the sound, and when it ceased I said, "Loon."

"Eyah," said Vic.

After another pause Vic said, "What-cha cookin'?"

"Nothing," I said.

Vic withered me with his aw-come-on-now stare, and his expression accused me both of lying to him and failing to trust him. Sort of—you can trust old Vic, you know, perhaps it's illegal? "Nothin'?" he said.

"No, I'm not cooking anything."

After a bit, "Lobsters?" he said.

"No. I'm not cooking a thing." I put on more wood.

"Clams?"

"No. Nothing."

"Getting ready to cook something?"

"No."

Vic stayed around, trying to see through my steam, and then he said something about a skiff that he thought might have washed ashore and he walked down the beach. He came back to stand around and hem and haw, and when I asked him about the skiff he didn't seem to recall anything about a skiff. He started off once, wagging his head, and then he turned back.

He said, "I don't know what you're doing—but if you don't put more water in that pot you'll be down to plain salt." He walked away. That was a lot of fun, baffling old Vic. Worth another try.

Ocean water, I decided, is considerably more salty than maple sap is sweet. At least a tablespoon of salt from a tumblerful. Such salt is impure and wholly unrefined, but it would cure fish and it was used in a day before the refinements of the pure-food laws. I had a cotton bag of salt from my experiment. Come August and humid weather it caked into a rock. Then, although I rinsed it well in fresh water, Mother's preserving kettle soon took on pockmarks and then rusted through. Now I remembered that Grandfather said the cauldrons were made of *copper*.

But even so, the experiment was worth-while. Vic told about it all around. "Mighty suspicious-looking when I found him, I tell you! Boiling a Methodist hell under a potful of nothing, and wouldn't speak a word about it. Mighty odd, I thought."

So I took my rich inward dividend when people came to ask, "Just what *were* you cooking?"

TWENTY-SIX

N ot too many people, even in Canada, know very much about Napoleon Comeau. Which is a shame. During the late 1800s and into the 1920s he became legendary in that remote and austere region called the North Shore—north shore of the St. Lawrence River. A man of numerous and amazing talents, he wrote a book called, simply, *Napoleon Comeau's Book*. I read it long ago with pleasure at his stories and amazement at his easy English prose—he didn't hear a word of English until he was eleven, and his total schooling came to ten months. Besides his native French, he also had Montagnais Indian. Somehow, on his own, he mastered enough of medicine so he was compared to the legendary missionary Dr. Wilfred Grenfell, and he doubled, without ordination, as a short-frocked priest to the scattered people of his rugged region. His father had been a post factor for the Hudson's Bay Company, which made a policy of moving its people every four or five years. Napoleon was born at an H.B. post at Jeremie Islands, off his North Shore, and his mother told him he had been found near the river alongside a salmon— the stork never got that far north.

Napoleon Comeau remains the leading Canadian naturalist. He, in turn, served as a post factor, custodian of fishing rights for the dominion and for the province, caretaker for the God-bout River fisheries, and just about everything else from post-master to coroner. A couple of stories from his book, summarized, should convince that it is worthy:

A Frenchman living alone on the North Shore heard noises during a vicious blizzard, and went out to stand in the night and gaze over the river he could not see. He heard men calling for help, and realized a vessel was in distress, but there was nothing he could do. By morning the storm had ceased, the sky was clear, and there was no ship in sight. But the shoreline was littered with debris from a shipwreck, and the man was able to salvage, among other things, twenty-seven hogsheads of Holland gin.

When Napoleon Comeau, at eleven, went five hundred miles upriver to attend school in Trois-Rivières, he found that the Anglican vicar who lived near the school had an excellent patch of melons. Surprised by the vicar while snitching a melon, Napoleon was forthwith yanked into the vicarage, into the presence of two pretty girls just his age who were eating popcorn. "I'm sorry, young man," said the vicar, "but I can't introduce you to my daughters for you haven't told me your name."

I had accordingly long had a hanker to go up to the North Shore to see the places told about in this book, and perhaps to meet somebody who would remember the man and could talk about him. There came a day, and my wife and I crossed the Saguenay River on the ferry to Tadoussac, and kept driving east until we came to a roadside sign that said Post Jeremy—Birthplace of Napoleon Comeau. And not too far beyond that we came to Baie Comeau, which I had supposed was to be a small waterside town where I might find *un vieux* who could recall Napoleon, for whom the place was named. Well, we had been driving for hours without a sign of a house, and who would expect to find anything up there but a small village? Driving into Baie Comeau was like driving into Bridgeport, Connecticut. It is a major city. Traffic lights are synchronized; the taxis, even back then, had radio dispatch. People up there fly, and the Baie Comeau airstrip was busy. The stores were smart, and the Hudson's Bay store was a whopper. I did inquire about Napoleon Comeau, and decided nobody in Baie Bomeau had ever heard of him. We rode over towards the pulp and paper mill with its mountain of pulpwood, and could see why Baie Comeau was a prosperous community. We also rode around the water front, and we came to a park which had a statue in prominence. When we came closer, the statue was a magnificent thing. The sculptor had caught the strenuous action of a birch canoe plunging down a rapid, the man in the stern alert and ready, paddle poised. Who could he possibly be except Napoleon Comeau? We left the automobile and walked closer. Now we could see the infinite detail of the artistry. The stitches in the birch bark, the root windings along the gunwale—all perpetual in durable bronze. There was a packsack forward in the canoe, and across it a deer rifle. And who do you suppose the paddler was in this tableau? He was Col. Robert Rutherford McCormick, owner and publisher of the *Chicago Tribune*. The plaque said this was to memorialize a man who had brought prosperity to the North Shore and to whom everybody in Baie Comeau would be everlastingly in debt.

I looked this up first chance I had. Born into the *Tribune*, McCormick came to own it after he earned his colonelcy in World War I. In his program of "vertical integration" of the *Tribune*, to make it self-sufficient, he had gone up to the North Shore, where he had roughed it as a boy and young man, with an empire of his own in mind. Starting with hydro-power development, he created Baie Comeau by building the paper mill. *Tribune* vessels took *Tribune* newsprint upriver and through the lakes to Chicago. Not one word about Napoleon Comeau.

The Boston Veteran Journalists' Association was founded before the memory of Man, and met once a year on the Saturday evening after the fall elections. The place was Mother Parker's Boarding House, and the purpose was to discuss clinically the way the Boston papers—of which there were then many—had handled the campaigns. In time Mother Parker's became the Parker House, and the postelection discussions became dinner meetings with anecdotal reminiscenses. Besides, the Boston newspapers dwindled, and those that were left stopped using journalism and took up something else. I was a member in good standing, and in 1962 served as president.

Before that, in 1954, Daniel J. O'Brien, Sunday editor of the *Globe,* was president, and the annual dinner was held on Monday, October 25, to accommodate a most distinguished journalist who was to deliver the address of the evening—Col. Robert R. McCormick of the *Chicago Tribune.* Living up here in Maine as I was, I didn't always go to the meetings, since it meant something of a trip and a hotel room for the night, but I certainly wasn't going to miss this one. I hoped I might have a chance to visit with Colonel McCormick a moment or two and round out the story of Baie Comeau. Mother Parker had a room for me, and at the proper hour I descended to the mezzanine to find the veteran journalists assembled around the flowing bowl in the customary meeting room—the same as for the last hundred years. I had just passed the door when Danny O'Brien appeared, grabbed my arm, and said, "I'm sure glad to see you!" He dragged me along.

"I'm glad to see you, too. Where're we going?"

"To the head table—you're the speaker of the evening!"

"What about McCormick?"

"The bastard isn't coming."

"What happened?"

"I don't know. Fifteen minutes ago I got a telegram. I suspect he never meant to come."

∽

Here at home, these years later, I cherish a silver Paul Revere bowl by my elbow as I sit in my ease of an evening and read a book. I keep it full of walnuts. Don't spill my walnuts, but if you pick it up you will see some engraving:

JOHN GOULD
AUTHOR AND JOURNALIST
WITH OUR APPRECIATION
BOSTON VETERAN JOURNALISTS' ASSOCIATION
OCTOBER 25, 1954

It is the bowl that was meant for Col. Robert R. McCormick of Baie Comeau and Chicago. And another time around I'd like to have a little more to do with Comeau, and a lot less with McCormick.

TWENTY-SEVEN

'Twould be absurd to wish for some things again. There was the time I made the trout chowder for the fish-and-game club. That was a one-time-only. Had to be. I was invited to tell some whoppers to this fish-and-game club, and I told them about Winnie Raymond and his trout chowder. Winnie was one of the original game wardens when Maine first set up a conservation department, but he didn't see any future in that so he went to guiding. He was one of the regulars at the old Kennebago Lake Club, and one of the best. Most of the old-time guides, the good ones, had certain parties they cared for year after year, and one of Winnie's was the Atwoods. The Atwoods were classic anglers and spent every minute out on the pond. They thought they couldn't fish without Winnie.

For a long time the trout chowder was standard noontime fare at Kennebago. Sometimes, by arrangement, several boats would come in to the same lunchground and a big pot of chowder would be made for the crowd. The thing about a trout chowder is its delicate flavor—otherwise it's made like any fish chowder. The guide—or guides—will dress the trout, tie them in a cotton cloth, and steam them over a pot of hot water. Just enough so the skins can be rubbed away and the bones picked free. This way, you have a dish of clear-quill trout meat and you set it aside. The pot is now used for the chowder, and into it goes the diced salt pork to try out. When you have fat enough, you retrieve the scraps to be served later atop the chowder, and you dump diced onions into the fat. When they get far enough along you add the diced potatoes. How much of each? Enough. Slap on a cover and let the onions and potatoes get acquainted with the salt-pork fat. A can of evaporated milk gives a chowder body, but some fresh milk is advised—depends on whether you want a loose soup or a thick one. Don't forget to dump in the trout meat. Like any fish chowder, this one needs to simmer, and the longer it simmers the better. The best chowders get made one day and served the next. But at the Kennebago Lake lunchgrounds, the chowder got made and devoured in the noon hour, and with the Atwoods, they didn't like to allow even an hour.

They wanted to get out on the pond and fish. So they pressed Winnie to hustle his chowders, and one day Winnie decided he'd had enough of *that*. He rowed the boat in, helped his "sports" ashore, brought in the basket, made the Manhattans, kindled his fire, dressed his trout, mixed the corn muffins, set the picnic table, and in exactly fifteen minutes the Atwoods sat down to their trout chowder. And as Sam Atwood stirred into his bowl with a spoon, up from under rolled the eye of a trout, which gazed at him sadly and then rolled back under.

Having made his point, Winnie said, "That's my fifteen-minute chowder," and the Atwoods never again pressed him for speed on the lunchgrounds. Shortly, Winnie was taking a full hour.

Well, the members of this fish-and-game club, perhaps because the club was downstate, hadn't heard of a trout chowder, and my story about Winnie brought on some questions. I told them if they'd stage a trout hunt along in May, I'd come and make them a Kennebago Lake trout chowder. This came to pass, and I arrived at the clubhouse shortly after noon on the appointed day. I found salt pork, onions, potatoes, milk, and biscuit materials aplenty on hand, and a note saying everybody would be in about four. They were out whipping the brooks, taking the trout. Fine. That would give me time to simmer the chowder, and we could have supper about half past six or so. I fixed the salt pork, cut up the onions, and diced the potatoes. I greased a biscuit tin and mixed my dough. Along about three I kindled a fire, meaning to have the range hot when I needed it. Then I walked out to look things over.

The clubhouse was on a fair-sized pond, and there was a good sandy beach. Looked to me more like hornpout water, and I guess it was. A small brook made up into a shady logan just east of the clubhouse, and as I stood looking at it I heard running water. About fifty feet upstream the brook became quite lively, and another fifty feet or so beyond I came to a beaver dam. I judged there was quite a flowage, and as I looked, a trout broke water. I said to myself, said I, that this would make a fine place to exercise a Professor, and made a resolve to do so in the near future. I went back to the clubhouse.

The boys came back an hour early, and as I saw the first arrive I thought this meant they had had good luck. It didn't. Nobody had had luck, and discouraged, they had all quit early. Fifteen men brought back three trout—one of them suspicious under the six-inch law. Glum was the word. When all the boys were back and we knew the total catch was three, I said, "Let me have a fly rod." You can depend on it—I didn't go directly to that beaver dam. I knew well enough by now that these boys didn't know the dam was there—right in their own back yard—and I wasn't about to rat on any beavers. I went in the other direction, circled through the woods, and came to the dam by stealth. It was a cinch. My first cast took a trout, and I got another on my second. Now, in a beaver flowage like that it sometimes happens that a school of trout will lazily swim in a circle, around and around the pool, feeding as it goes. So after two, I didn't take any for a time, and then on the next passage of the school I took five. In a little over a half hour I had twenty-three trout, all in the ten-inch range. I went back to the clubhouse by my previously described devious route.

"At least," I said, "you boys can dress 'em out."

There was never, even before creation, such silence as I got the rest of the day. Many and many and many a time I, too, have come back empty-handed. That's no shame. In fact, the contemplative angler may not even fish when he goes fishing—there was one magnificent time when I came upon a fox den and I went to sit in the shade of a pine and watch for action. The vixen came out with her four pups and played with them, rolling and kicking, and they never knew I was there. Fishing is what you make of it. And fisherman's luck is fickle. My going for trout that day at that dam, on the basis of my having stumbled on it, made a sure thing. But why volunteer information?

"Where'd you get *them?*"

"Skill," I said, "will tell."

And then all this big silence. It was a superb trout chowder, partly because I made them wait an extra hour for osmosis to set in. They were patient, because they remembered about Winnie Raymond and the Atwoods. But nobody talked. Everybody just sat, looking off into space, and a monumental wonder hovered over all. It was, and you know it, a dandy thing for me. I hummed and stirred chowder, and kept an eye on the biscuits, and otherwise joined wholeheartedly in the silence.

But it can't be done again. A year later I went back to that beaver dam. It was still there and the beavers were still active. I cast out and had no reply. I stood there two hours and caught nothing. There wasn't the slightest evidence that a trout had ever resided at that address. I suppose they were still there, but I chose the wrong day. Not feeding. No chowder tonight. No repeat.

TWENTY-EIGHT

A boy's first feed with the men in a Maine lumber camp would be worth another, except that the real old-time Maine lumber camp isn't there any more. I was about fifteen or sixteen, and although the lumber camp that entertained me wasn't far up in the Maine wilderness—it was far down in York County, near Alfred—it was authentic in its own time. This was in school vacation and I had been treated to a few days with my maiden aunt. She was Aunt Lillian, and afterwards retired after forty years as deputy clerk of courts for York County. Alfred was the shire town. Her small home was just off the rear door of the courthouse, and she knew every lawyer and judge—as well as every plaintiff, defendant, and witness—who passed that door. She was a little bit of a body, devout and proper, and had one of those photographic memories, with complete recall. A lawyer would call her on the telephone to say he had a case that revolved around such-and-such a point, and could she help?

"Oh, yes—now, let me think: In 1884 Judge Martin ruled on that in the May term, and found for the defendant."

But in my aunt Lillian's life there were few things to absorb the attention of a fifteen-year-old, and a visit to her by any of her many nephews and nieces petered out after a day or so into the doldrums. There were a few things to be seen in the courthouse. The oldest records in Maine are there, and some of the Indian land deeds have been mounted for permanency and are worth a look. Aunt Lillian had also culled some humor from real-estate descriptions that were amusing. One deed began "at the tree where we hitched the horse," and another one said, "on this side of the above described line." I remember the courthouse janitor, Mr. Rankin, was also a barber and had a chair in the basement corridor. This moonlighting on county time was chiefly to oblige lawyers and judges, so Aunt Lillian considered it all proper. She had a little lecture she gave me that if I lived an honest and upright life, studied hard, and kept good table manners I might grow up so I could sit in the judge's chair with honor. She considered the practice of law a notch and a half above the Christian ministry, and she hammered this at me so persistently that I was rather grown up before I recognized that lawyers are crooks and judges are their assistants.

Aunt Lillian did have the gift of narrative and a fine sense of humor. But it didn't take her long to run through the history of Alfred, and it was always nice, when visiting her, to go home again. But she knew this, and did her utmost to keep us amused. For me, she arranged a visit to a lumber camp. From 1939 to 1948, Raymond E. Rendall of Alfred was forestry commissioner of the State of Maine. This is not a political sinecure; it is one of the most important positions in the Maine government. It calls for executive ability and a working knowledge of timberland management. The rangers and wardens make a considerable force to be directed both in law enforcement and fire control, and the commissioner needs tact and judgment towards timberland owners and industries. Also, a hefty part of Maine is in various lots, parcels, islands, and townships set aside under his management—certain preserved wild lands. I think Mr. Rendall was not a distinguished commissioner, but he was adequate and better than average. He was, first of all, a forester, and before he became state commissioner he had an office in Aunt Lillian's Alfred and managed certain timberlands in York County.

In the history of Maine, the forester stands high. Both in the days when Maine was part of Massachusetts and after it was set off as a separate state, great tracts of forest were sold, granted, and even stolen, and the ultimate owners of such wild lands needed men to handle their affairs. The Kennebec Purchase of William Bingham, a Pennsylvania merchant, ran to a million acres; in all he came to own some three million acres of Maine. Bingham lived in Philadelphia and came to Maine just once to see his property. So he employed foresters, and they set the pace for the traditions of Maine timberland management. Some lands were granted to educational institutions, income to be used for endowment. The Bowdoin College Grant, for one, was sold off to private owners and the money was invested for future reference, but while the college owned the "wild townships" she had foresters to manage them. Today, the towns of Foxcroft, Guilford, and Abbot stand on the Bowdoin Grant. Bates College, however, was a come-lately in the culture of Maine, and wasn't around when public lands were being passed out. It was the Maine State Seminary with Baptist blessings in 1855, and was chartered as Bates College in 1864. But there were some later bequests of real estate to Bates, so that she, too, came to need foresters. Some of the holdings were in York County, and Mr. Rendall of Alfred became a Bates College forester. Aunt Lillian asked him if he didn't have something going on that a boy my age might enjoy.

I have the notion that in Alfred my aunt Lillian's wish was everybody's command and so Mr. Rendall, while he would rather have done just about anything else, agreed to take me out to see the lumbering operation on the Bates College lots. Mr. Rendall, Aunt Lillian told me, would take me to see the sawmill. This was to be on the Saturday. So I looked at the old deeds one morning and watched Mr. Rankin barber a judge in the afternoon, and the next day I sat in the judge's chair up in the courtroom and was told that with diligence and probity I might one day sit on the Supreme Court, and Saturday morning finally arrived. Mr. Rendall jingled up to Aunt Lillian's door with a horse and sleigh.

Aunt Lillian had me ready, and I slid under the buffalo robe with Mr. Rendall and off we hied in high adventure.

It was early in the morning, right after an early breakfast, and it was February—Washington's Birthday time—so the morning was sharp. But the sun is getting ready to climb March Hill by February, and the morning moderated. It would be a lovely day, soft air and the feel of maple-sugar time. As we trotted along, wet places appeared in the road, where snow was melting. Soon we left the public road and started up a two-sled road into the

Bates lands. There we would inspect the cuttings, collect the scaler's slips, compare his figures with the sawyer's total, confer generally with Mr. John Stevens, who was the *entrepreneur de bois* of this operation, and dine in state with the lumbering crew in the camp cookshack at noon.

In the early days of hauling logs, the butts were chained to a bobsled, and a team brought them out with the top ends dragging on the snow. This was a "one-sled," and it could operate on a rudimentary road, or even on no road at all. Later, two such sleds were chained end to end to form the traverse-runner rig known as a "two-sled." Now the whole log was sled-borne. This was easier on the horses, but it did require a reasonably good roadway. A "two-sled road" simply meant a road where logs were hauled on a two-sled—it never meant that the road was two sleds wide. On this one, into the Bates lands, our little sleigh was riding in the tracks made in the spring-soft snow by the great runners of the logging rigs. We were going along with our runners deep in trenches. But—O! Boy-o-boy!—the two-sleds were drawn by a team, while our single horse had to walk up in the middle on a crown that was treacherous.

(Author's gratuitous addendum: There was—but Mr. Rendall didn't have one—a vehicle invented in northern Maine for just such situations. It was called a set-over pung, and it had the fills—the thills, or shafts—to one side, so the single horse could step in the path made by the off horse of the team. Had Mr. Rendall owned a set-over pung, this episode in the Bates timberlands would not have been so memorable.)

Our horse, quite naturally, stepped off to the side so he could walk handily in a team track. The runners of our sleigh then fetched up against the trenches in which they were moving, and over we went. It happened quickly. The horse side-stepped, crunch went the runners, up went the sleigh, over went we into the snowbank. The horse stopped, we righted the sleigh, got back in, and before long the horse side-stepped again. Remember how the White Knight in *Through the Looking Glass* keeps falling off his horse? We made like the White Knight all the way into the Bates cutting. Good that the day had come off warm, because we were soaked with snow water. To me, this was something of a peril, but to Mr. Rendall and the horse it appeared to be customary procedure for wood-lot inspections. Certainly Mr. Rendall was as unperturbed as any White Knight, and not once did he ask if I was hurt, or even scairt. *Ça va!* We arrived, much bumped and very wet, at the lumber camp.

This was before chain saws, and the men were felling trees with crosscuts. We passed some choppers (in the Maine woods, even though he uses a saw, the man who cuts down trees is a "chopper") before we came to the buildings in the clearing, the sawmill, and Mr. Stevens. When I was introduced, John Stevens said, "Oh, Lil's nephew!" and I was surprised at this—I supposed everybody in Alfred called her Miss Gould, as did all the lawyers. A man led our horse to a hovel, and we walked about with Mr. Stevens, who had a scaling stick and kept clapping it to the butts of logs. "Bad heart up this ridge," he said, and I saw a good many discarded logs with hollow centers. As we went along, from all sides came, now and then, the yell of *"Timber-r-r-r!"* and a tree would crash. It was a cutting of good-sized white pine, and I was thrilled to see the snow cascade into the air when a tree came down *ker-smoosh.* At one time Mr. Rendall showed me the way to take a board-feet scale—a very close estimate of how many board feet the sawyer will get from a log—but that's the only lecturing I got about timberland management. It came time for dinner and the gong was heard.

The best eating houses in Maine have always been the lumber camps, and for good cause. Remote, the early camps depended on dried and salt meats, routine beans, and often locally taken fish and game. Trout and venison, while excellent now and then, cloy with repetition. Chopping is hard work and makes appetite. So a lumber-camp cook had to be a genius, as day after day he had to satisfy the crew with foods tastily prepared from improbable beginnings. It is true that in the early days of long logs an experienced woodsman wouldn't sign on until he learned who would cook. The camp of Mr. Stevens was typical enough of the Maine kind. Take all you want, but eat all you take. The boiled tea was rugged and hot, and thick from evaporated milk. Two kinds of meat. Boiled potatoes with plenty of gravy. Turnips, squash, and carrots. The cook, arms folded, stood back to watch the men file past for cafeteria service, and at a snap of his fingers the cookees would refill the platters. After the men were at table, the cookees brought replenishments as needed. The sweets were on the tables—several kinds of cookies, squares, plain and jelly doughnuts, pies, cakes, gingerbread. Then the fruit, bowls of tinned peaches, pears, pineapple, and stewed prunes. The adamant Maine lumber-camp rule of "no talk at table" was relaxed somewhat on account of me. Everybody spoke, tousled my head, and those near me at table kept passing me things with, "Have some?" But Mr. Rendall and Mr. Stevens, while they talked business down at one end, observed the rule enough so they spoke in whispers. I took a biscuit, broke it in two, and laid on some butter. A man across the table reached over and drenched the two pieces with molasses. I nodded, and he smiled. I ate beyond my need and my capacity. As the men finished eating, one by one, they rose, gathered up their dishes, and carried them to the sink. I did the same—a required routine I was to perform many, many times afterwards in many, many other Maine lumber-camp cookshacks, but I never had a better meal than that one. The cookee would wash the dishes, but not until the men brought 'em in. I said to the cook, "Some good!" He thanked me. Mr. Rendall and Mr. Stevens were still talking, so I wandered outside with the men, and sat with some of them in the good February sun on the platform of the dingle. The cook came out and handed me a paper bag of molasses cookies.

We White Knighted all the way back to the public road, and what drying off we'd got at the lumber camp came to naught. I was soaked again. It was still daylight when he let me down at Aunt Lillian's, and when I thanked him for a good day he said, "That's all right." Mr. Rendall, I believed, was somewhat pleased to see me off his back. He drove off. I told Aunt Lillian that the day had been great, and I meant it, and I gave her the bag of molasses cookies. She feigned pleasure and said, "Oh, isn't that nice!" but Aunt Lillian was the molasses-cookie champion of our whole family, and this was coals to Newcastle. But before bedtime that night we had one of the lumber-camp molasses cookies apiece with a glass of milk, and she had to admit they were all right. "Identical!" she said. "Identical!"

I didn't see Raymond Rendall again until 1939, when he was sworn in as forestry commissioner. He didn't remember me when I appeared to congratulate him. But then he said, "Oh, yes—Lillian Gould!" He broke into a grin. "I was scared to death," he said, "that you'd go home and tell your aunt how I bounced you out of that sleigh. You could have been killed."

"I never mentioned that," I said.

"Well, that explains why she never did either—but for some time I expected she'd light into me."

TWENTY-NINE

I t's well to stick to your trade, but my only foray into the mysteries of the theater was, I thought, a dramatic success, if a dismal failure. Knowing nothing about plays and playwriting and play-acting, as an art, I was drawn into this innocently by my penchant for helping everybody. Our schools had an English teacher who was far better than the average, and we always felt a bit sorry for her. Our town was not all that culturally oriented, and let us say the funny books outsold Dickens and Swift. She tried, and was casting her seeds on stony ground. One of her jobs was to coach dramatics for the annual one-act-play contest. This gaucherie came once a year when schools of the larger area sent teams to compete, as in basketball and baseball, and there was supposed to be some high-brow value to the winning school. Our teacher said the talent supplied her by our lackluster community was hardly of competitive quality, and her biggest difficulty was getting youngsters interested in trying out for parts. Besides, she was of the same opinion as me—that Thespian activities ought not to be like shooting off a pistol and holding a foot race. Somehow, in our conversations I volunteered and thus became the assistant coach for the next one-act-play contest. This teacher said another problem was finding a suitable play; the business of supplying plays for such contests seemed to be tied up in a publishing house that—I concluded after looking at a few samples—must have been owned by idiots. I could see why interest was lacking. We, clearly, had to find something else, and something better. Something to bring our youngsters in and keep their interest. Something, that is, that would be fun. I remembered from my college French *The Farce of Master Peter Pathelin.*

Written in the 1400s by an unknown French author, the text wavers toward the end and the dialogue is sketchy. But several have tried to develop endings, and in 1872 an Édouard Fournier brought off his complete version in modern language. This is what *The Oxford Companion* says about the farce:

> Pathelin, the lawyer, tricks the close-fisted Joceaume, the draper, out of a piece of cloth. Joceaume presently discovers he is being defrauded by his shepherd, Aignelet, whom he hales before the judge. Aignelet consults Pathelin as to his defense. Joceaume, confused at seeing the rascal Pathelin in court, mixes up his two complaints, against the lawyer and against the shepherd, and is recalled to the business of the moment by the judge in the famous phrase, 'Revenons à ces moutons'. Aignelet, who to every question replies, in accordance with Pathelin's advice, by merely bleating, is discharged as an idiot. But the tables are turned on Pathelin when, in reply to his demand for his promised fee, Aignelet merely bleats.

I worked the Fournier text, with three or four days' attention, into a version which I thought would suit our purposes and which, fortunately, has been lost. The stenography class at the school made copies of it for the cast, with relatively few mistakes. I thought it wasn't all that bad. It was in down-Maine Yankee now, anyway, and when I read it to a group that was "interested in the stage," it even created excitement. The big thing, of course, was the humor—it was going to be fun to do, and nobody ever yet in the history of the one-act-play contests had had fun. I did, or at least tried to, impress the youngsters that comedy was difficult—more difficult than tragedy—and I remember quoting that eminent authority Molière: "Making people laugh is a strange business."

Perhaps in its own way this was one of my most enjoyable deviations. We hoakied the thing to the hilt, in which embellishment we had the help of my friend Dr. George Rockwell, the retired vaudeville actor, who taught us how to walk, how to emphasize certain words, how to wait on effect, and all the tricks of his trade that would not be in the bag of an English teacher. Doc said to find a sheep.

We found a sheep with a lamb. We kept them in a cage at a distance, and when the lamb was brought onstage at rehearsals it would bleat for its mother, and then it would bleat some more when Aignelet bleated. Since these interruptions couldn't be foreseen, they put the youngsters on their own with a good many ad libs—not always the same twice—and we whipped that ancient farce into a fast-moving laugher that at least would amuse the crowd, win or lose.

Our big scene was the opening of court. To give you an idea: First, a kazoo band playing the March from *Aïda*, supported by a Boy Scout color guard and a platoon of Girl Scouts selling cookies. Next, Hizzoner in robe, with flower girls scattering rose petals ahead and a page boy on behind holding his train. As the judge appeared, six heralds blew trumpets offstage. The judge was followed by a sort of French Revolution rabble, these to be the spectators in court. Then came Aignelet, lamb under his arm, with a sign that read JUDGMENT IS NIGH. And so on, until the rear was brought up by a man pushing a cart and selling hot dogs and sody pop. Master Pathelin had his best day in five hundred years, and the lamb bleated magnificently. The audience howled in delight, the only happy audience in the history of the one-act contest.

In these contests the winning play is selected by a judge sent around by the Maine Principals' Association. Our English teacher told me I shouldn't expect too much. She knew. After the several plays had been presented, this judge came on the stage to offer his comments on the productions and to award the trophies. The first thing he did was to disqualify *Master Peter Pathelin* because we had used a live animal in the cast—animals, he said, always steal the show and this is unfair competition in a dramatic contest. Then, which certainly taught me a good lesson, he said he preferred, anyway, to have the prizes go to serious works which were done in a studious manner, rather than to frothy efforts intended only to amuse. I sat there with the horrible awareness that here was a teacher of dramatic arts, licensed to teach in our public schools, acceptable as a judge of stagecraft by the Maine Principals' Association, and he had never heard of *The Farce of Master Peter Pathelin!* ''The most famous . . . ,'' the book says.

For only one reason would I subject my self to a repeat of my dramatic experience: I neglected to catch that chap's name, and on the next time around I would set it down as that of a public-school-system fathead.

THIRTY

T rue, it was willy-nilly. But it is so. Briefly, I was a bootlegger back in the golden days when Maine ran heavily to
bootleggers and rumrunners. The prohibition amendment was
supposed to wean a thirsty nation, but the State o' Maine rallied
wholeheartedly to frustrate this noble intent. A substantial prosperity set in along the down-east coast which ended with repeal.
Pity. The long Maine shoreline with its inlets and islands was
much too much for the revenuers to patrol, and as almost anybody with a good boat became a rumrunner, so did others
become bootleggers, and in a smooth if illicit manner the palates
of many good citizens were assuaged unconstitutionally. The
occasion when I joined, innocently, in the transportation of illegal alcoholic beverages was when the rumrunners of Maine col-
laborated, around 1920, to lick the United Mine Workers, who
were on strike. Coal was scarce, Maine was having a hard winter, and an uncle of mine, who was a coal merchant, decided
something had to be done.

I didn't know that my uncle was a bootlegger. It was something he shielded from public knowledge. It was sort of a side-
line with him, and if anybody asked him what business he was
in, he would mention fuel unless you winked and put one thumb
in your mouth. Being but a lad then, I didn't realize that his
handsome Hudson Super Six automobile was a vocational
touchstone—the number of Hudson Super Six automobiles in
Maine which were not owned by bootleggers was minimal. It
was a heavy vehicle, with ample inside space, and it would hold
to the dirt roads of that decade at high speeds, so that enforcement officers seldom caught one in the act.

As to fuel, the oil burner was in the future, and Maine
depended on coal. When the Mine Workers went out on strike,
the coal pockets of Maine began to run low, and as cold weather

continued, a crisis was upon us. Some schools had to close, factories went on half time, and homes closed off rooms. My uncle, having a considerable community to serve, gave the situation thought and decided he could do something about it. He looked into the coal matter, and learned an interesting thing: With the miners on strike, an emergency existed, and the protective tariff was relaxed. So long as the strike continued, foreign coal could be brought into the United States duty-free. My uncle's next step was to bring in some foreign coal, but he wasn't enough of an operator to bring it in all by himself. A shipload of coal was beyond his finances and more than he could handle. The answer was a co-operative purchase. I didn't know anything about all this until some time afterwards.

My uncle thereupon got in touch with the principal coal merchants in all parts of Maine, asking if they would participate in a joint purchase. All of them wanted to, and the only objection came on financing. Some of the smaller dealers couldn't swing that much at once—which made sense, because this deal would pretty much mean Maine's coal for a year. The next thing was to make arrangements for the financing, and my uncle (by now aided by two–three other coal dealers) went and called on some bankers. The bankers of Maine have never won any significant prizes for positive thinking, and since this kind of proposition had never come along before they were leery. Within the next week or so my uncle and his friends had seen most of the bankers, and while there was some willingness to put up a little money here and there, the total was insufficient. A fine idea was about to wither and die.

My uncle then gathered together his colleagues in the rum business. One by one he found them here and there, and stated the case. Some were down the coast waiting for shipments; some were in Providence and New Haven making collections. In just a few days he had cash collateral enough to back twice the resources of every bank in Maine—his bootlegger friends being more than willing to take 10 percent of Maine's yearly coal bill for such a small favor. This in hand, the next thing was to gather together everybody necessary to bring off this large and somewhat complicated deal. The date was set for a certain Saturday, and the place would be the offices of the Pocahontas Fuel Company on the Portland waterfront. Pocahontas had the wharf and facilities for unloading ships, and had a spur track from the Portland Terminal Company, so coal could be reshipped by rail to the dealers throughout the state. On that Saturday would assemble the coal dealers, their lawyers, the shipping agents, the customs brokers, the railway officials, the bankers, the insurance underwriters, the import company representing the Russian interests that would supply ten shiploads of anthracite over the next three months—and the bootleggers who came in their Hudson Super Sixes to cosign the notes.

That Saturday morning I was at the post office when my uncle drove up in his Hudson Super Six to pick up his mail. While he was in the post office I was admiring his automobile, and when he came out he said, "Want to go for a ride?"

Thus I attended that meeting in the offices of the Pocahontas Fuel Company. My uncle parked his Hudson Super Six with deliberate care so it stood a little apart from the other Hudson Super Sixes—and after the meeting I was to learn why. We went in to find a considerable company and there was a good deal of handshaking. Soon a man stood up and tapped his jackknife on a desk and said, "Gentlemen, I'm sure we're in complete agreement, and binding the bargain shouldn't take long." Papers passed around, and everybody signed four or five. That was it. The whole purchase, from coal mines in Russia to the farthest kitchen range in Aroostook County, was sewed up in about fifteen minutes. My uncle and I came out to find a rear door of his Hudson Super Six standing open, and a man beside it.

"All set?" asked my uncle.

"All set," said the man.

My uncle brought out his wallet and gave the man quite a few bills; the man counted them, put them in his pocket, and then turned to go. My uncle looked in the Hudson Super Six and said, "You might have put the seat back."

The man didn't say anything. He just walked away. I got in and saw that a number of square five-gallon tin cans had been neatly fitted into the space under the rear seat. The rear seat cushion was still tipped up. I fitted it into place, and then got in the front seat beside my uncle. We drove along.

So I knew how the bootleggers of Maine kept the state from freezing to death, and I participated in illegally transporting intoxicating beverages during the golden era of the rumrunner. Some years later, after the prohibition amendment was repealed, I asked my uncle about some of his adventures, and he had one story worth adding here:

With his Hudson Super Six loaded with cans, he was on his way to a delivery, and an automobile pulled out of a side road as if to stop him. He shot off the road and around the car, high-tailing it away. He was now pursued by, he presumed (and rightly as it turned out), the law. Off he went, and behind came they. It was nip and tuck for a time, but the Hudson Super Six had the heft and the speed, and even though loaded with the cans it was able to pull away. But then the police must have used a short cut, because there they were again. Two or three times he thought he'd lost them, but again they'd appear. The chase lasted over an hour and ripped over back country roads my uncle never knew about. At last he seemed to be alone, but he had no idea where he was and his gasoline tank was low. He didn't relish the thought of being stranded in unknown territory with so much evidence. Maybe, he thought, he ought to stash his cans in the woods before his gasoline was all gone, and drive ahead far enough so nobody would guess where the cans were. While looking for just such a good chance, he rounded a turn and came upon a country garage with a gasoline pump. Even better, although it was now after midnight, an electric light was burning. He pulled in.

A woman in night clothes and a robe came from the house, and my uncle asked her if he could get some gasoline. "Certainly," she said, and she filled his tank.

Gasoline was not expensive then. Even a Hudson Super Six

could have its fuel tank filled for two or three dollars. The woman replaced the cap and my uncle handed her a twenty-dollar bill.

"It's two seventy-five," she said.

"That's all I've got," said my uncle.

"Well," she said, "I'll have to go to the house for change. My husband can make change. He just got home. He's a deputy sheriff and he's been out all night chasing a rumrunner."

"Keep the change," said my uncle.

THIRTY-ONE

For a few years after I brought my bride out of the comforts of Massachusetts to endure the rigorous disciplines of a farmer's wife in Maine, we were visited now and then by friends of her girlhood who were curious as to how she was making out. One of the great joys of my life has been her recurring "Thank you for bringing me to Maine"—something she says when she sees a bluebird in the hollyhocks, or the first snow on Mount Katahdin, or a red lobster just out of the pot, or a gaggle of geese on the—her—shore, or something like that. Sometimes she just says it. Her girlhood friends naturally supposed we were living in a wigwam with dogs that howled all night, and they approached the journey up Route 1 with the intrepid fortitude of a Marco Polo tackling the Gobi Desert. They were astonished that we had a telephone. These visits gave us a chance to display the hidden charms of the State of Maine, and we had many a good time with her pals and their spouses. When Roy and Mildred MacDonald came, we took them up to New Vineyard to see Chesley Pinkham.

It's been some time now since we called on Chesley, and I've been thinking we ought to do it again—if we can find the place. His story begins about 1791. In the late 1700s some of the women on Martha's Vineyard, southerly from Massachusetts, decided they had endured enough of the hardships and sorrows of island life. The Vineyard, Nantucket, and New Bedford area was but a gateway to the sea, and every day women wept as news, or no news, came. These women wanted back into the country, as far from the ocean as possible, and as a consequence a group of about a dozen Martha's Vineyard men bought a wild township in Maine called Number 2—west of the Kennebec River and north of the Plymouth Patent. Shortly some seven families came with all their possessions in oxcarts, making a wagon train for which, in places, roads had to be cleared. The destination was a rocky ridge running east–west from the Sandy River to the Carrabasset River country, and to reach this unpropitious granite the carts crossed the fertile Sandy River valley—Maine's best farmland bar none. The river, 'twas said, looked to them like water, and the women said, "Push on!" On the ridge, where the seven families took up seven farms, each one a mile from the next, there was certainly nothing to remind of the bounding billows of the Atlantic. This community never prospered, but by hard work and by doing without it survived, and its people became the ancestors of just about everybody north of Skowhegan, Madison, Farmington. After they had been there some years with fields cleared and homes tight, they made arrangements with Chesley Pinkham to come and be their miller.

There was a north–south road into the upper Carrabasset country, coming up from Starks through what is now called West Mills, and then going through a bog towards the present site of New Vineyard village—the present New Vineyard being then nonexistent. This road crossed a small brook coming off the mountain, and immediately on the north side of this brook the road ran up the ridge to the seven farms. This is where Chesley built his mill. He put up a dam with a small penstock, erected the mill, and geared his saw and his stones. He was to be the miller there even after the original settlers waned. He was the only person in the community who had never seen Vineyard Sound. Chesley, unlike the poor farmers, prospered. People came from considerable distances to use his services, so he wasn't dependent on the New Vineyardites alone. He, 'tis said, never married, was socially a recluse, and was fiscally a miser. After many years he converted his miller's share into double eagles, the gold coins set at twenty dollars. Using an auger the right size, he bored holes somewhere in the timbers of his mill and dam, fitted the coins in, and plugged the holes. Since carpentry was then done with treenails, plugs in timbers meant nothing special, and nobody knew except Chesley where he had done his banking.

So, late in the 1800s, after the seven original settlers had waned somewhat, there came a hell-twister of a spring rainstorm, the brook rose fearfully in the night, and Chesley's mill went tumbling down over the ledges into the valley below. Timbers were strewn in the woods along the bank for miles. For years after that Chesley wandered up and down the stream, looking, looking, looking, and as nobody knew about his treasure the people assumed he was crazy and let him look. Eventually, however, Chesley told—else we wouldn't have the story today—and after that just about everybody wandered up and down the stream, looking and looking. Not a trace of Chesley's gold was ever found. It's still there, somewhere, awaiting discovery. And, down on Martha's Vineyard off Massachusetts, some people will tell you, Captain Kidd once buried some of his treasure. Captain Kidd and Chesley Pinkham!

You'd have to know that country pretty well to be able to go in there today and find any traces of the original New Vineyard. One by one the houses fell into the cellar holes, and forest trees grew from the cellars. For a time there were lilacs and grapevines to show where dooryards once flourished. Here and there would be a "spoolbush," the shrub that every colonial home grew by the back doorstep. It was pithwood, and by punching out the center a woman could make a spool for thread and yarn. The home of Chesley Pinkham, latest come, was latest left. Porcupines were still chewing on it, but there wasn't much left, in the 1930s. There is nothing by the old roadway to indicate that a mill ever stood there. Instead, there is one of the most beautiful brooks in Maine, coming off the mountain as always, and cascading from pool to pool down over a mile or more of granite ledge. There are some trout, but small—the pools are nurseries for fingerlings that move down into the valley as they grow. Just below the site of Chesley's mill the stream divides and makes an island of a granite shelf—to my mind the finest picnic spot short of Eden. It was to this lunchground we took the Mac-Donalds to tell them about Chesley Pinkham.

The day was a dream—October and fallish, but comfortable.

The maples were at their best. The brook was neither high nor low—just right—and we could step across onto the ledge. We rearranged the little stones of the picnic fireplace and prepared to ennoble and exalt the beefsteaks that had accompanied us. We had about everything anybody needs on this kind of time, with a splendid Gravenstein apple pie to punctuate the climax. The stream rippled, gorbies came and spoke to us at great length about many things, the wood smoke lingered to perfume the scenery, we were alone, the ghost of Chesley Pinkham attended, and our friends from Massachusetts were beginning to suspect that some of this, at least, was real. When the onions that were to adorn the steaks began to waft their salubrity in all directions, my attention was distracted from the frypan by a remark from Roy, who was lolling back in an attentive but relaxed posture.

"Oh, oh!" he said. "Here comes trouble!"

I had to turn to look up towards the old roadway, towards the site of Chesley's one-time mill. And here was nothing to get excited about, and it certainly didn't mean trouble. We were having a visit from the game warden. Down he came to step over to our ledge, prominent as a midnight fire in the scarlet jacket then official uniform in the Maine hunting season. His name was Bell; he was district warden out of Kingfield. He had been going about his district posting signs that read Don't Shoot—It Might Be Your Sister! in the manner of the warden service, getting ready for the deer season in November, and he had chanced our way. From Roy's way of speaking, I had an insight as to life in Massachusetts. The law is the law and an enemy. Contrariwise, in the Maine woods the law is an ever-present help in trouble, a true friend, and (it proved true now) good company. Roy thought we were about to be arrested for something—trespass, maybe. He said afterwards he was relieved when I said, "Well, welcome, Warden—come share our humble meal. Have you got your deer yet?"

Warden Bell said he wouldn't trouble us except perhaps for a slice of that there pie. "Apple, I judge," he said. But he managed to get a piece of beef down after the pie, and a rod of johnnycake, and two cups of coffee, and another piece of pie. Roy and Mildred simply stared bug-eyed at this tilt with the law, and when Warden Bell found out he had a couple of folks "from away" for a captive audience, he gave out with all stops open. Roy and Mildred went back to Massachusetts knowing a good deal more than they did when they came up to Maine to see us—and some of it was true.

When we had packed our things back in the automobile, and when Warden Bell had reluctantly gone, I turned toward the Pinkham place, and called, "Well, good-by, Chesley—see you next time around!" But for some reason I can't account for, we haven't been back to New Vineyard since.